TWAYNE'S WORLD AUTHORS SERIES
A Survey of the World's Literature

HUNGARY

Enikö Molnár Basa, American University

EDITOR

Ferenc Molnár

TWAS 574

Ferenc Molnár

FERENC MOLNÁR

By CLARA GYÖRGYEY
The International P. E. N. Club

TWAYNE PUBLISHERS
A DIVISION OF G. K. HALL & CO., BOSTON

Published in 1980 by Twayne Publishers,
A Division of G. K. Hall & Co.

All Rights Reserved

Printed on permanent/durable acid-free paper and bound
in the United States of America

First Printing

Library of Congress Cataloging in Publication Data

Györgyey, Clara.
Ferenc Molnár.

(Twayne's world authors series ; TWAS 574 :
Hungary)
Bibliography: pp. 186–91
Includes index.
1. Molnár, Ferenc, 1878–1952
Criticism and interpretation.
PH3288.G9   894'.511'23   79–2546
ISBN 0–8057–6416–X

For my family: Mother, Ferenc, Kati, and Mari

Contents

About the Author

Clara Györgyey was born in Budapest, Hungary. She earned an A.B. and an M.A. from the University of Budapest, both in English and American Literature, and then an M.A. in English Education from Yale University. She is presently serving as a Master Teacher of Modern European Literature and Drama for the Yale Teacher Preparation Program at North Haven High School, working on her dissertation. She has adapted five plays into English, among them *Catsplay*, which is still running in several theaters in the USA and Europe. She has translated four novels and two film-scripts from the Hungarian, and has authored more than 150 articles and essays. Mrs. Györgyey is the President of International P.E.N. Club's American Exile Branch.

Preface

Molnár, already a legend in his lifetime, epitomized all the virtues and defects of his work. His paradoxical personality and his works alike evoked extreme emotions. Throughout his career, he was besieged by ardent admirers and fanatic enemies. He split the camps of critics both in Hungary and abroad; at the summit of his success, each Molnár play was greeted with sound and fury, with panegyrics and scorn. His friends and foes were equally vocal and passionate in their attempts to define the author's unprecedented popularity, but their temporary evaluation was always charged with emotions and often motivated by social and political reasons, subject to changes in accordance with the intellectual climates of the successive micro-eras. As a result, no comprehensive biography or objective critical analysis of Molnár has ever been written. This study has been undertaken to redress the inordinate subjectivity of previous critics and at least to fill partially the lack of critical evaluation of Molnár. The recent revival of interest in Molnár's work further inspired this study, originally prepared as a modest tribute to the author when the hundredth anniversary of his birth was celebrated. With the passage of time, more valid judgment of Molnár's art has emerged since the reaction of posterity is often the only true test of prominence.

During my research, I encountered numerous difficulties: despite Molnár's wide publicity, accurate information and data concerning his long and colorful life are scarce. The writer himself had been extremely secretive about his private life; for example, no reference book mentions the names of his parents and not even his grandchildren could supply this simple information. Most of his contemporaries have died, and a great deal of resource material in Hungary was destroyed during World War II. In addition, obtaining the prolific writer's seventy-two volumes was no easy task. Furthermore, writing a book about a Hungarian author for an American public presented special problems. Hungarian is an isolated language; its culture and literature are relatively unknown in the English-speaking world. Thus, I could not assume familiarity with Molnár's background and native idiosyncracies on the part of the reader, nor could I suppose that the interested students and scholars had had a chance to view his plays in America between 1908–1930, when Molnár was one of Broadway's most popular playwrights. Perhaps the severest limitation was the realization of the enormity of his artistic output and the relatively little space at my disposal. Since I aimed at rendering the first complete evaluation of Molnár's literary career, I was unable to analyze every work in depth. Instead, I chose to discuss all the novels, plays, and collected volumes of the most representative shorter pieces fairly briefly, devoting more or less space to individual works according to their significance.

Since Molnár was an autobiographical artist, all his works are here presented closely intertwined with historical and biographical comments, necessary extensions of the cursory introductory chapters which describe his milieu and his life. In discussing his works, I adhered to chronology within those chapters which are arranged according to genres, covering his achievements in the fields of journalism, short story, novel, and drama. His masterpiece, *Liliom*, warranted deeper analysis, and so did his unfamiliar late writings during the final years in the United States. Therefore, these were treated in separate chapters.

While writing the book, I have tried to maintain a reasonable balance between plot summaries and critical commentaries, and provide the Hungarian and American views alternately, bearing in mind both those readers who are totally unfamiliar with the author and those who merely seek new insights for a better understanding of him. I feel I have been able to offer a general exposition to Molnár's *oeuvre*, a useful resource book, and a challenge for further study.

Whenever the work under scrutiny was available in translation, I quoted the authorized English text, even when it was not accurate or the style of the adaptation seemed inferior to the original. In these instances, however, I made an effort to warn the reader who, in all probabilities, would have access only to the English versions.

Preface

In the preparation of this critical evaluation I have been motivated by two convictions: first, that an objective, succinct analysis of all aspects of Molnár's life and works may shed a new light on their inextricable interrelationship; and second, that the accomplishment of the Hungarian "King of Entertainment" is worthy of listing in the annals of world literature.

CLARA GYÖRGYEY

Orange, Connecticut

Acknowledgments

I wish to thank the Molnár family and the executors of the estate for allowing me to study the Wanda Bartha Collection at the New York Public Library in Lincoln Center; and John Pauker for granting me access to the Pauker Deposit at Yale University. I am grateful to Irodalomtörténeti Intézet, Szinháztörténeti Intézet in Budapest, and the Yale Drama Library for the generous permission to use their research material. I would also like to acknowledge my indebtedness to Professors Manuel Duran, E. J. Gergely, Sarolta Kretzoi, Emil Lengyel, George L. Nagy, and Péter Nagy for their advice and extremely valuable suggestions on revision, to Miss Patricia Jordan and Mrs. Susan Lengyel for their assistance, and to Professor Enikö Basa, my editor, for her patience and good counsel.

Chronology

1878 Born in Budapest on January 12, the second son of Dr. Mór Neumann and Jozefa Wallfisch.

1887– Attends Református Gimnázium (high school) in Buda-
1895 pest.

1895– Studies law in Budapest and Geneva; travels to Paris;
1896 becomes a journalist, returns to Budapest; changes his name to Molnár.

1898 Death of mother; travels in Europe; publication of *Magdolna*.

1901 Publication of first novel, *Az éhes város*.

1902 Opening of first play, *A doktor úr*, in Budapest.

1906 Works for *Budapesti Napló*; marries his editor's daughter, Margit Vészi.

1907 Daughter Márta is born; publication of *The Paul Street Boys*; opening of *The Devil* in Budapest.

1908 Death of father; *The Devil* is performed all over Europe and in New York; election to Petőfi Society.

1909 Production and failure of *Liliom* in Budapest; long illness.

1910 Divorces Margit Vészi; *The Guardsman* opens in Budapest.

1911 Attempts suicide; convalescence in Austria. Election to Kisfaludy Literary Society.

1912 *The Wolf* opens in Budapest, two years later in New York. Publication of two short story collections.

1914– War correspondent on the Galician front.
1915

1916 *The White Cloud* wins the Academy's Voinits Award; war diary and volumes of essays published; awarded the Franz Joseph Order.

1917 Opening of *Carnival* and *Fashions for Man*.

1920 Opening of *The Swan*.

1921 Opening of *Liliom* in New York.

1922 Marries the celebrated prima donna Sári Fedák; *Heavenly and Earthly Love* opens in Budapest, *Fashions for Man* in New York.

1924 Divorces Sári Fedák; opening of *The Glass Slippers.*

1926 Marries actress Lili Darvas; *The Play's the Thing* opens in Budapest and New York.

1927 Awarded Legion of Honor after *The Swan's* Paris premiere; first trip to USA on Dec. 22; President Coolidge receives him in the White House.

1928 *Collected Works* in twenty volumes published in Budapest; opening of *Olympia.*

1929 Opening of *The President*; publication of his play collection in English, *The Plays of Ferenc Molnár.*

1932 Meets Wanda Bartha; travels in Europe, opening of *Harmony* and *Arthur* in Budapest, revival of *Liliom* and *The Good Fairy* in New York.

1934– Continues traveling in Europe with Wanda Bartha; four
1936 new plays open in Budapest.

1937 Opening of *Delilah*; leaves Budapest for the last time.

1940 Arrives at New York on January 12; moves to the Hotel Plaza, where he stays till his death. *Delicate Story* opens in New York.

1943 Suffers a massive heart attack.

1945 Publication of *Farewell My Heart* and *The Captain of St. Margaret's.*

1947 Becomes an American citizen; Wanda Bartha commits suicide.

1948 Refuses to return to Hungary for the celebration of his seventieth birthday. His health begins to fail.

1950 Publication of *Companion in Exile* and *Stories for Two.*

1952 Dies in New York of cancer, April 1. Publication of *Romantic Comedies.*

1955 Sári Fedák dies in Budapest.

1961 Margit Vészi commits suicide in Spain.

1974 Lili Darvas dies in New York.

CHAPTER 1

Molnár's Budapest

I The Era

HUNGARY, a small country in the Mid-Danubian Basin, flanked by various Slavic peoples on one side and Austro-Germans on the other, has survived for a thousand years among her formidable neighbors. Hungary's linguistic isolation and suppression by more powerful neighbors explain why its literature and culture have been virtually unknown to the world up until the twentieth century. Since even the most cursory summary of Hungary's history would be too complex to include here,[1] the following concise historical overview covers only those years that were most formative in Molnár's life: the *fin de siècle* epoch, when his literary career began, and the first two decades of the twentieth century, when he was Budapest's leading dramatist. Only a brief outline is given of the period between 1920–1940, when Molnár, living abroad, only visited his native land.

A long period of struggle against foreign domination and domestic oppression came to a close at the end of the nineteenth century with the Compromise of 1867, when the Dual Monarchy of Austro-Hungary replaced the monolithic Austrian Empire. This brought momentous changes in Hungary and remained the basis of the social and political fiber for the next half century. The political and social structure of the country remained outmoded and feudal, but its economy underwent profound changes as capitalist progress gathered momentum.[2] Industry expanded on a large scale, creating a rapidly growing working class. Social insurance was extended to workers; compulsory education was introduced and health services were improved. Despite the emigration of hundreds of thousands, there was a marked population increase. Industrialists and merchants prospered, and unprecedented wealth accumulated in segments of a new middle class

17

aggressively seeking power and seizing the economic and political leadership, which was slipping from the upper class. Urban population multiplied, and Budapest became a cosmopolitan city.

Although the government managed to maintain order, crucial political and social problems remained unresolved and tensions persisted behind the deceptively unruffled surface. The Compromise provided only a tenuous feeling of independence: the dominating influence of the Austrian "partner" persevered, a reality bitterly resented by most Hungarians craving for complete freedom. Furthermore, the Monarchy ignored the problems of the sizable minorities (Slovaks, Croats, and Rumanians), who had no political representation and whose social and economic status was considerably lower than that of the Hungarians.[3] The agricultural problems also remained unresolved. Hungary was basically still an agrarian society; the largest segment of the population (72 percent), the peasantry, was impoverished. Its living standard was woefully low and changed very little while the urban population profited from the gradually developing industry and trade. The aristocracy still owned most of the land, and since the peasants provided an almost inexhaustible reserve of cheap labor, the nobility made no effort to increase productivity or introduce mechanization. This blatant exploitation compelled countless peasants to seek a better life abroad while disaffection was mounting among those who remained at home.

In this relatively peaceful period, the country celebrated the thousandth anniversary of its existence. The millennium year of 1896 brought Hungarians into a state of euphoria: national pride overcame dissatisfaction and prodigious celebrations were attended by enthusiastic millions. Under the glittering facade the underlying conflicts seemed to have vanished in the atmosphere of jubilant optimism. But, after the feast the fast: early in the twentieth century hidden discontent surfaced, further aggravated by political crises in leadership. There were two sharply divided factions. The conservative group, as strident as it was powerful, advocated extreme nationalism; the liberal faction, determinedly fighting for progress, was disorganized and weak and unable to muster sufficient support for its program. The split caused general confusion. The country was engulfed in political nepotism, corruption, and an overall deterioration of morality in all spheres of public life.

In this era of social disorder and political chaos, Prime Minister Count István Tisza emerged as a stout defender of "law and order," a code name for the status quo.[4] His remedy was to continue his father's paternalistic rule in the rural regions while allowing the cities to "glut themselves on *laissez faire*."[5] Conservative and stubborn, Tisza nevertheless put through some moderate reforms which created more favorable conditions for the working class and peasantry while providing additional aid to free enterprise and boosting business ventures. Tisza's strong will guaranteed a temporary stability during which considerable social and economic progress was made, but the outbreak of World War I buried all these reforms.

Hungary's participation in the war was both catastrophic and absurd. Why should Hungarians take up arms to die in order to avenge the assassination of a Habsburg? While hundreds of thousands of Hungarian soldiers fought in foreign lands for an alien cause, their country all but disintegrated. Devastating poverty, worsened by the costly war, and news of heavy casualties and inevitable defeat on the front led to fierce antiwar protests. General discontent with the political leadership and clandestine reports about the Russian Revolution made people realize that drastic changes were imminent. All over the country tension was mounting: workers went on strikes and violent demonstrations erupted in the cities. The left-wing and Socialist ideologies steadily gained momentum. The old Emperor died and his successor, Charles IV, was powerless to act. Tisza was forced to resign in 1917. The following year the front collapsed. Hungary lay in shambles: the government became panic-stricken. The revolution broke out.

The Habsburg regime was succeeded by the democratic government of Count Mihály Károlyi, who proclaimed a Republic on October 31, 1918, and became Prime Minister on November 2. He proposed radical land reform and urged the signing of the peace treaty. Yet he lacked charisma; he was incapable of coping with the tremendous multileveled pressures tearing at the country. In the midst of total confusion, bitterly disappointed, he yielded his power to the Left, led by Béla Kun, the

Communist commissar.[6] On March 21, 1919, the Dictatorship of the Proletariat was declared; in his role as Foreign Minister, Kun proclaimed Hungary a Soviet Republic where the power rested in the hands of Soldiers', Workers', and Peasants' Councils. Kun's regime stifled every opposition with terror. However, not even the iron-fisted commissar could withstand the invading foreign armies which gathered to occupy Hungary. When the Rumanian armed forces reached Budapest, Kun resigned and fled, handing over power to a Socialist Democratic government. But this rule too ended in confusion on November 16, 1919, when Admiral Miklós Horthy marched his troops into Budapest. The proletarian dictatorship was completely crushed in the three months following the flight of Béla Kun.

In 1920 Horthy was elected Regent Governor of Hungary and in the same year the Trianon Peace Treaty imposed upon Hungary was signed at Versailles. The treaty deprived Hungary of approximately two-thirds of her former territory, and 59 percent of the population. Also, industry and commerce were critically impaired.[7] Events of this period signaled the end of "greater" Hungary.

The Horthy regime was characterized by political extremism of varying features. Though Horthy was head of State, the actual power rested in his Prime Ministers' hands. Noteworthy among these Prime Ministers was Count István Bethlen. A man of great integrity, he gradually restored stability and legality in Hungary. With the help of foreign loans, he curbed the paralyzing inflation following the war and, in 1925, introduced a new currency, the *pengő*. But, during his conservative regime, chauvinism, mixed with anti-Semitism, spread in the country. Restlessness flared up in the ranks of the proletariat, both rural and urban. The middle class began to disintegrate, immersed in internal political squabbles. Hungary lived in a condition of growing skepticism mingled with increasing apathy; her social troubles were aggravated by the Depression that hit the world in 1929.

Bethlen retired in 1931, and the thankless task of steering Hungary in the years of economic crisis was assumed by Count Gyula Károlyi, soon succeeded by Gyula Gömbös. An uncritical admirer of the totalitarianism of Hitler and Mussolini, Gömbös openly stood for Fascism. His ideology assumed significance when he hit upon the idea of gearing his foreign policy to what he called the "Rome-Berlin Axis." Gömbös concluded a long-term trade treaty with Germany, making Hungary subservient to the German economy. Toward the end of his regime, native Nazi groups began to surface and anti-Jewish legislation was introduced. This policy resulted in an alliance with Nazi Germany. By 1937–38 it was obvious that the world was on the threshold of a new war which Hungary had every reason to dread. It was at that period when Ferenc Molnár left his native city, Budapest, for the last time.

II *The Roots—Molnár's Budapest*

Molnár had all the makings of a cosmopolitan. He grew up with the Hungarian capital. As Budapest changed into a vibrant European metropolis from a provincial Eastern European city, Molnár became a leading figure in the international theater world. Though he had achieved worldwide fame, his roots rested in the native soil. Throughout his life, the wanderer Molnár was never able to assimilate successfully to any other culture and held out as a thoroughbred Budapester, an epitome of the spirit of the Hungarian capital.

Budapest formally became one city in 1873 with the merging of Buda, Óbuda (Old Buda), and Pest. The two main parts, separated by the Danube River, represented the duality of the nation: Buda built on hills, flanked by forests and protected by citadels, was all ancient glory topped by the Royal Castle overlooking the Danube; and Pest, built on the plains, urbanized at a frantic speed, adorned with modern boulevards and apartment buildings, was the site of the impressive House of Parliament, ministries, stock exchange, museums, and universities, and was the center of culture and business. Buda, the bulwark of tradition, and Pest, the vanguard of revolution, combined the national characteristics of the country, a synthesis of aristocratic and democratic aspirations. As the journalist Ignotus so well expressed it, "In her social and architectural foundations she took after Vienna, in her cravings for wit and grace she

imitated Paris, but in enterprise and sensationalism, she resembled New York."[8]

Late in the nineteenth century, when the capital began
developing, the predominant language in Budapest had been
German. Soon, however, the upwardly mobile bourgeoisie
emerged as ardent patriots who spoke and wrote in Hungarian,
making the city a stronghold of Magyarhood. A new heterogeneous class structure also emerged: merchants, artisans, and officials
of German origin, urbanized Hungarian gentry impoverished by
the economic changes, industrial workers and the elite among
the peasants, and finally, the Jews.[9] Molnár was born to such a
Jewish bourgeois family.[10]

Undoubtedly the most important element in this middle class
was the fervently assimilating Jewish population. Its recent im-
migration was accelerated by the decree of full emancipation
enacted soon after the Compromise.[11] In the leadership of the
city the blend of Jewish intellect and Hungarian gentry proved
felicitous, complementary to each other: the gentry, being conservative, adhered to the old; the Jews, being liberal, embraced
the new. The two groups provided a wholesome balance in
their common goal: elevating Budapest from provincialism and
changing it into a modern city. The latter constituted most of
the trading and professional middle class, and were the fore-
runners in establishing new branches of industry. The majority
of cultural and literary leaders were also Jewish. As Ignotus
noted, they were the instrumental force in turning Budapest
into a cosmopolitan city and paving the way to the Golden Age
of literature of the first decade of the twentieth century.

The general rule was that, above the cobbler's and locksmith's level
and outside the gentry caste, membership of the middle class—of the
Burgerschaft, or bourgeoisie, or, in Magyar, the polgárság—implied
Jewishness either of faith or origin.[12]

Many Jews were converted, changed their names, and otherwise fortified their assimilation by marrying into old Hungarian
families. Paradoxically, they became even more zealous Magyars
than many gentile Hungarians. Molnár was a typical product of
this patriotic generation of Jewish intellectuals, not only forging

ahead at a rapid pace but also dictating attitudes, literary style, and artistic taste.

Although the more philosophical writers were deeply involved in Germanic thought, the dominant intellectual influence came from France. Paris held Budapest in the spell of her charm and made the Hungarian capital the Eastern depository of French *esprit*. The pulsating French literary cafés had their replicas in the Danubian metropolis, where the air was filled with cosmopolitan spirit. Hungarian writers and artists frequently visited Paris in search of new themes and new modes of expression striving to catch up with the West. After returning to Hungary, they disseminated the French spirit and translated and promoted French literature. Soon Zola's naturalism and Baudelaire and Verlaine's symbolism were adopted and emulated by the Hungarian literati; there were Magyar counterparts of the Parisian cabaret and new boulevard comedies pervaded the Hungarian stage.

In 1896, when Molnár embarked on his literary career as a journalist, the capital had already entered the industrial age and was on her way to becoming a modern city. The rest of the country, still in the grip of semifeudal conditions, could not keep pace with the capital. The striking dissimilarities were apparent and the widening economic gap between cities and the countryside became even more pronounced. The ambitious middle class was aggressive in dictating trends and attitudes, often stifling the ambitions of the provinces. The country gentry and the peasants, in turn, vehemently resented the new radical tone emanating from Budapest, a city they regarded as a "nest of aliens," allegedly opposing traditional Hungarian values. In turn, the "sinful" city intelligentsia, mainly responsible for generating the changes, regarded the country folk as backward.[13]

Additional unrest was fermenting within the capital. The growth of capitalism produced a fast-increasing industrial working class seething with discontent and getting organized for the protection of its interests. In a city where materialism dominated, where values were measured by money, the conspicuous inequalities aroused envy and hostility among the workers; clashes were bound to happen. The majority of the proletariat lived in extreme poverty. This poverty, though, similar to the misery of landless peasants, seemed even more intolerable because of the indifference and impersonality of the big city. In rural communities life was somewhat more humane and family relationships were closer-knit; in the shabby urban ghettoes the destitute belonged nowhere except at a favorite tavern or café. This alienation and the visible contrast between their wretched lives and the glamour of the prospering bourgeoisie inspired the workers to fight for economic advancement and for a share in political leadership. Thus, the new middle class was pitted against both the demonstrating and striking proletariat and the country nobility. These phenomena were by no means typically Hungarian: other urbanizing European countries had experienced them also, except that in most of Western Europe these changes had taken place much earlier, more gradually, at a less hectic pace.[14] At the early stage of his career, Molnár was acutely aware of these social conflicts and regularly exposed them in sharp editorials and essays.

In this tension-ridden atmosphere different groups of men of letters emerged and vastly diverse literary clubs were organized. Molnár's regular clubs were the "Fészek" (Nest) and "Otthon" (Home). They launched newspapers and magazines portraying Hungarian life according to their ideologies and life-styles. Most political parties and social circles had their own press organs. Budapest was tolerant; at the cafés the spokesmen of arch-conservatives, moderates, Socialists, liberals, and Marxists argued for their causes. The leaders—Molnár among them—were mostly journalists by profession, working for various publications, because at that time in Hungary it was difficult to eke out a living "merely" by writing novels or poetry. Molnár's favorite "Café New York," a glittering rococo structure, was the scene of many ideological disputations. It was also his observation post, working place, and audience chamber. The same "Café New York" was the headquarters of most of the other outstanding literati who paved the way to the Golden Age of Hungarian culture.

III *The Renascence of Hungarian Literature*

Between 1890–1900, newspapers and periodicals were the pioneers of the ensuing cultural rejuvenation. First of the trend-setting publications was the weekly review *A Hét* (The Week), edited by József Kiss. Established in 1890, it performed a historic role of uniting a heterogeneous lot of writers, Christians and Jews, conservatives and liberals, who wrote in a modern, urban tone, employing a polished literary style not exempt from Budapest colloquialism. While *A Hét* had no radical program it did oppose provincialism. The witty, entertaining articles of high standards reflected the capital's sophistication and held up a mirror of Budapest to the countryside. This innovative journal was the pivot of some of the dominating literary currents of Europe. It provided a forum both to apprentice writers, who ruthlessly mocked stuffy conventions, and to the established authors who were less violent in denouncing "establishment" and less prone to break with literary traditions.[15] Kiss, an exceptionally able editor, succeeded in satisfying the taste of the urban middle class without alienating the good will of either the aristocracy or the gentry. His bipartisan stance was exemplary and he trained scores of fine journalists (Molnár among them). *A Hét's* effect intensified the urge among the literary leaders to create new and daring novels and plays.

In the next decade intellectual activities quickened as new talents emerged. The demand for progress and revival was not confined to literature. Philosophy, science, art, and music also began to flourish. An enumeration of the works of art, scholarship, technological innovations, and scientific findings dating from this period would add up to an impressive total.[16] All these movements had one common goal: to launch a modern intellectual renaissance characteristically Hungarian, aligning it with the mainstream of Western culture, probing the cultural and social values, discarding anachronistic ones, strengthening constructive insights.

The struggle for revival in literature was fraught with contradictions as the different trends (Naturalism, Impressionism, Symbolism, and Expressionism) reached their syntheses in the works of young writers. These currents eventually were reinterpreted through the Magyar psyche and the Hungarian language. However, the changes often occurred too late. By the time these authors had given the new ideas their accolade, most of them were no longer "new" in Western Europe. Thus, the "modern" Hungarian works were not innovative enough to affect, let alone penetrate, other cultures. Nevertheless, the achievements of this generation were unique, unparalleled in Hungary's history. They were pioneering ventures of the Hungarian literary Renaissance.

The mainstays of the reformist-modernist campaign, under the guidance of new *animateurs*, Ignotus and Ernő Osvát, were eager to launch a high level, Western oriented magazine, a forum of their own. After some unsuccessful ventures, the Ignotus-Osvát group finally started a literary journal *Nyugat* (West), in 1908. "This date," Péter Nagy pointed out, "marked the beginning of the revolution which radically changed the Hungarian literary scene, not only through the talents it revealed, but also and mainly by the effect of their revelation. . . . [*Nyugat*] stood for social progress, large cities, democracy—modernity and modernism in all the accepted meanings of these terms."[17] The contributors freed Magyar literature from parochialism. By refurbishing the national heritage, incorporating the most highly refined foreign elements in their works, they made *Nyugat* truly cosmopolitan. Dozens of outstanding *avant-garde* poets, linguists, translators, and critics joined it, dedicated to the task of disseminating first-rate literature. Without yielding to various pressures, the editors championed full artistic freedom, aesthetic consciousness, and literary purity. They refused to discriminate among gifted contributors on the basis of their political convictions; they ignored conservative public opinion and the pressures of the Academy; *Nyugat* maintained its artistic autonomy even if it meant fewer readers—and less income. The *Nyugat* group gradually altered the course of Hungary's cultural life and their periodical remained influential for decades, though under successive editors and changed forms. Though Molnár never belonged to the inner circle of *Nyugat*, he expressed many of its ideas and ideals.

It must be noted that despite its remarkable effect, *Nyugat* had no particular social orientation. This small, exclusive group of intellectuals represented a rebellious segment of the middle class which had found a shelter in the art from their conventional bourgeois milieu: they escaped into artistry from the very class which they repudiated. But only a select few of the middle class understood and supported this elitist literature. The majority, the average middle-class person, frequented the conventional theater when in need of culture. The stage was their escape, their surcease: the plays suited their not too refined tastes and imposed little obligation of deep thinking on the audience. On the stage the spiritual revival was less esoteric than in the publications. Hungarian drama began to imitate certain extrinsic features of foreign models (Maeterlinck's Symbolism, Hauptmann's Naturalism) while otherwise staying unaffected by many burgeoning, innovative trends. Nevertheless, a few noteworthy changes did occur in this genre too. In the last decade of the nineteenth century new theaters opened and achieved instant popularity. In 1904 the Thália Society was organized to revitalize Hungarian drama in the manner of small theaters in Western Europe.[18] Emulating the goals of Paris's *Théâtre-Libre* and Berlin's *Freie Bühne,* the directors of Thália tried to cultivate realistic subject matters, artistic tone, and more naturalistic dramatic stage techniques. Meanwhile commercial theaters boomed, new types of plays were produced, and shortly it became the hallmark of *savoir vivre* to attend sophisticated plays. This atmosphere was propitious for Molnár, an enormously prolific playwright, whose ascent was spectacularly swift, who captured the proper tone, employed impeccable techniques, and at once, became Budapest's favorite dramatist. Soon after, as he became an internationally celebrated master of drawing-room comedies, Hungarian literature at last broke out of isolation and penetrated Western culture.

CHAPTER 2

Molnár's Itinerant Life

I The Man

FERENC Molnár was Hungary's most celebrated and controversial playwright; his personality and art perpetually elicited extreme reactions. His enthusiasts hailed him as the world's greatest entertainer, a second Molière; while his opponents chided his sentimentality and lack of substance with similar passion. During his lifetime he was one of the capital's most hated literary figures, yet, his works were secure bestsellers and his premieres drew the most ecstatic crowds in Budapest's theatrical history. Even after his death, so called "mock trials" were held in Hungary. Prosecutors and defenders were equally vocal and passionate in their attempts to redefine the author's popularity, which, to some extent, emanated from his charismatic personality. The omnipresent dichotomy of Molnár's artistic *oeuvre* was similarly revealed in his dramatic life-style, and, since a great deal of his personal traits were transmitted into his characters, a closer view of Molnár the man is warranted.

Molnár had an Oscar Wilde-like elegance; his air of distinction was accentuated by a monocle which he had worn since he was twenty years old. His impeccably tailored suits made him appear taller than he was. He was a handsome man, the paleness of his "moonlike" face contrasting sharply with a glow in moments of exhilaration. His dark eyes were luminous, with the radiance of intelligence and with glints of humor. He was the idol of many beautiful and talented women.

A true cosmopolitan, he was born to wealth and lived in luxury most of his life. Demonstrating his *carpe diem* philosophy, he was a hedonist: a connoisseur of good food, and a gourmet cook himself; a devotee of red wine, plum brandy, of espressos flavored with cognac; a chain smoker of his special brand of Turkish cigarettes. Above all, he was noted as a relentless lover of women. He cheated brazenly in his advanced age when doctors enforced a strict diet and abstinence.

Molnár was a bibliophile: he read three or four books a day and his palatial library in Budapest contained over 5,000 volumes in *de luxe* bindings. He was fluent in German and French (and learned English late in his life), well versed in Italian, Finnish, Greek, and Latin, and able to quote long passages in all these tongues. He was an avid reader of newspapers, too, and was phenomenally well informed about current affairs. Molnár was also an accomplished musician—an amateur composer and critic; he played the piano, violin, and cello; he was reputed to have a fine singing voice. He sketched skillfully, and not only designed some of the settings of his plays, but also drew character portraits. Molnár was a confirmed hypochondriac; his almost paranoiac fear of death and pain explains his keen interest in medical science and the occult. He believed in omens and magic numbers. He hated telephones, crossing streets, and wasting money. In fact, his parsimony was as legendary as his wit.

His real genius was revealed in conversation. A verbal wizard at puns, axioms, and bons mots, he became the undisputed head of a group of talented artists who followed him in the cafés and clubs of Budapest. Celebrated writers and theatrical people coming from abroad considered it a privilege to call on Molnár and seemed to enjoy his sardonic wit. His searing sarcasm spared neither friend nor foe. His spontaneous vitriolic put-downs were often followed by tenderness and remorse. And people forgave him because, as one of his critics observed: "the mocker was a darling of the people, a true social lion.... His social charm was such that his epigrams became public property, as if he were the 'Joseph Addison' of the local intellectual aristocrats."[1] Also, the inimitable raconteur jester was always ready with riposte; few individuals or institutions were spared by his lance, dipped more often in pity than in gall. His scintillating improvisations seemed almost too overwhelming; it was regretfully stated later that "had he written it down instead of talking it away in all-night carousals, we should have had volumes of brilliant humor."[2]

Yet, Molnár's sophistication was a mask for his sentimentalism, skepticism, and all-enveloping cynicism. Despite the all-night fireworks, Molnár managed to stay aloof and disclosed little of his private personality. Underneath the pompous facade, he was vulnerable, vain, hypersensitive, and in need of unremitting applause. One of his translators, Benjamin Glazer, commented about this duality: "His dread of failure hampers him. An odd situation, truly, and in some aspect a tragic one. Genius lacking the courage to spread his wings and soar. A potential immortal bidding fearfully for the praise of a café-house clique. Is it vanity? Is it abnormal sensitiveness?"[3]

Molnár's dual nature was even more manifest in his relationships with women. Albeit he had a mordant humor and a debonair stance, he was insecure and often shy, suffering from the effect of deep-hidden remnants of sibling jealousy and severe depressions. In his much-publicized dramatic love affairs and marriages, he was mean, domineering, possessive, and neurotically jealous. Like his character Liliom, Molnár vacillated between cruelty and repentance; posing as a romantic lover, he often inflicted pain. Adrift between passionate love and despair, incapable of changing his ways, he was unaware of the damage caused by his egocentricity and conceit. From the festering wounds of his marriages and liaisons the author gathered strength to populate his stories and plays with couples frequently engaged in the battles of the sexes, as he had been. Like most other artists, Molnár, too, transposed his own inner conflicts into his art.

In the midst of the domestic dramas—usually caused by him—Molnár posed as if he were merely an uninvolved spectator who savored every minute of life's complications. On other occasions, he took shelter behind a shield of silence, observing people and events, carefully carrying out his perpetual quest of character and plot. He rambled about town, wandered from café to café, from one friend's house to another, from Turkish baths to clubs, but he seldom went home. There were times when he did not return to his apartment for two weeks. During these restless years his method of writing was rather unorthodox.

He might carry the seed of a play or novel for years, and when each angle had been thought out, he transcribed the entire work in a few days. In the course of such writing spells, he worked uninterruptedly for hours, without food or rest, until the manuscript was completed. Surrounded by swarming waiters, deafened by clattering dishes, unperturbed by the loud noise and the band music, Molnár would sit in a café all night, rapidly writing in longhand, his lettering immaculate, seldom correcting the manuscript. But when *Liliom*, the last play written this way, failed, he promised his first wife to abandon this method—the only promise, by Molnár's own admission, given to a woman that he ever kept.[4]

Since he aimed primarily at being an entertainer and not a preacher or propagandist, Molnár shunned politics. Although fully conscious of world events and the serious social and economic problems of his time, he deliberately avoided incorporating them into his works, except for a few early newspaper articles and short stories. While he may have sympathized with the underdog, Molnár remained a stranger to the real conflicts of the proletariat and the peasantry. He lived and worked in an hermetically closed bourgeois environment, and of the lower classes he mostly encountered only servants, waiters, coachmen, and beggars. Even when times became foreboding, before World War I and II, he continued producing romantic stories and plays of fantasy. As Gassner commented, "His life and work reveal everything that is characteristic of a theater that belongs to dramatic history as one popular way of coping with life—that is, sugar-coating it."[5] Adhering to his *carpe diem* philosophy in which the basic impetus for action was individual gratification rather than social, national, and economic responsibility, he created dramatic history by reducing world calamities into drawing-room strife. By the touch of his magic pen, Molnár always provided the public with escape, gaiety, and an illusory world in which conflicts were fun and amenable to solution.

Precisely because of his airy approach, Molnár became an easy target of critics. For the same reason, he emerged as a guru to his disciples, as well as a favorite author of millions around the world. The obvious dichotomy in his personality and works might explain why, on the one hand, he was extolled as "the

Hungarian Molière," "the sparkling Aristophanes of the cafés," "the monocled Swift of Budapest," "the Voltaire of the boulevards," and, at the same time, berated as the spoiled "Golden Boy of the bourgeoisie," a conformist who discarded his artistic responsibilities, prostituted his art for money and success, and who chose seasonal humor and schmaltzy sentimentality instead of substance.[6] The conflicting remarks warrant the conclusion that Molnár's universal appeal was not justified on either purely political, social, personal, or aesthetic grounds. A sober, unbiased evaluation has been long overdue.

II Early Years at Home

It was generally assumed that Molnár's life was public property, its details discussed or joked about by the Bohemians at the cafés. In reality, little was known of his childhood or youth, and for decades Molnár refused to write his autobiography. One of the club members remarked that Ferenc Molnár would never write his memoirs because he could not attack himself. Whenever the author was asked to describe his early life, he told a humorous anecdote or a caustic story of a trivial event in his childhood. Finally, yielding to pressure in 1925, he wrote a capsule "autobiography" in the preface of one of his books:

1878, I was born in Budapest; 1896, I became a law student at Geneva; 1896, I became a journalist in Budapest; 1897, I wrote a short story; 1900, I wrote a novel; 1902, I became a playwright at home; 1908, I became a playwright abroad; 1914, I became a war correspondent; 1916, I became a playwright once more; in 1918, my hair turned snow-white; in 1925, I should like to be a law student at Geneva once more.[7]

This list of biographical landmarks tersely summarizes the meteoric rise of his artistic career.

Ferenc Molnár, second son of Dr. Mór Neumann, a prosperous Jewish physician, was born on January 12, 1878, in Budapest. (The parents' favorite son, László, died a year before Ferenc's birth.) His mother, Jozefa Wallfisch, was a frail, taciturn woman, frequently bedridden, who died in 1898. His father, a popular gastroenterologist, had little time for his son; he was busy in his office during the day and spent the nights at the casino and the cafés. The household was opulent but gloomy, an air of illness permeating the somber rooms; it was not a friendly atmosphere for the lively and precocious Ferenc, who constantly had to be warned to keep quiet. "My birth was followed by a five-year hiatus," Molnár wrote in his capsule autobiography. The exaggerated fear of death and sickness Molnár displayed all his life may be traced back to these early years.

The birth of his sister, Erzsébet, in 1881, brought no considerable change in his life, and the overactive Ferenc's frustration was further aggravated by his tutors. For several years the Neumann children were taught at home, as was customary in patrician families at the time. The monotony of this existence was somewhat enlivened when Ferenc learned to read, marking the beginning of his long-lasting love affair with literature.

An eagerly awaited change in his life occurred in 1887, when he entered the Református Gimnázium (Calvinist Gymnazium). Among his teachers he remembered Ferenc Baráth in particular because he had urged his students to learn foreign languages by relating fascinating tales about other cultures. Molnár was so impressed that he began to study Finnish in earnest.[8] His writing talent was budding: at fourteen, on his own initiative, Ferenc started a periodical called *Haladás* (Progress), written in long-hand. It sold four copies. A few months later he launched another publication, *Életképek* (Panorama), which, in lithographed form, reached a circulation of twenty copies. Having found the newspaper business unlucrative, the imaginative adolescent undertook his first dramatic work. *Kék barlang* (Blue Cave), written, directed, and staged by Ferenc, was performed in the basement of a friend's house. It was about alchemy, and its major props—blue bottles—were filched from Dr. Neumann's office. The flickering candles in the bottles illuminated the stage with a mysterious blue light. The play must have been controversial because, as he tells us, "It ended in a riot. In consequence of which, my next play had to languish for a decade thereafter, until the Comedy Theater of Budapest saw fit to present it."[9]

After the completion of his secondary education in 1895, Ferenc enrolled at the University of Budapest to study law. It was at that time that he got into the habit of going to the "Central

Café" to do his assignments, and since he spent more time there than in the lecture halls, his father sent him to Geneva to pursue his legal studies there. During the two semesters at the Swiss University, following the advice of a family friend, Péter Heim, he began to write in earnest, sending home reports and sketches to various papers. He also found time to complete a short "novella," *Magdolna*. To polish up his French and to see some of the popular new plays, he went to Paris. The fashionable boulevard comedies of Bernstein, Bataille, Capus, and others left a deep impression on him and later greatly influenced his dramatic style. To the dismay of his family, Ferenc suddenly returned to Budapest. There he started to write regularly and changed his name from Neumann to Molnár. Since the articles sent from Geneva had found favor, he abandoned law as a career after a few abortive months of further legal studies, and became a full-time journalist in 1896, a year when he had his eighteenth and his country its thousandth birthday.

As a journalist, Molnár covered a variety of topics, but mostly court trials for Vészi's *Budapesti Napló*. At these hearings he became acquainted with the problems of both high society and the "lower classes." Also, he contributed fiction to other newspapers about various subjects, writing in a picturesque, colorful style which attracted instant reader attention. It did not take him long to acquire a "name."

Then he moved into an even more exciting field—fiction. His first full-length novel, *Az éhes város* (The Hungry City), was released in 1901. A bitter book, a scathing indictment of money-hungry politicians and social climbers, it portrayed the capital's unconditional surrender to an ambitious man who returned from abroad as a multimillionaire. This relentless *exposé* of the evil effect of money, viewed by a young, idealistic newspaperman, attracted considerable attention and made Molnár's name widely familiar.

The following year was particularly important in Molnár's literary career. He began writing for the theater, a medium through which he eventually became internationally famous. Most of his early dramatic pieces were a byproduct of his journalistic work. These plays had their inception in impressionistic sketches, random scenes and chronicles which had been written daily for the papers with no thought of ever developing them into full plays. Several of his columns included overheard or imagined dialogues. His first play, *A doktor úr* (The Lawyer), an amusing farce in the style of French comedies, had been conceived in this manner. His next comedy, *Józsi*, which reached the stage only two years later, had also been published as a series of short dialogues featuring an obnoxious youngster: a dramatization of newspaper sketches about a spoiled rich child.

During this period Molnár published at least one volume, and perhaps two volumes, of short stories, essays, and dialogues. His fame grew rapidly; his charm and banter, as well as his notorious love affairs, soon made him the favorite author of the bourgeoisie and the idol of the literary set which wrote, drank, and swapped gossip in the cafés.

In 1906, he was promoted to the editorial board of the *Budapesti Napló*. Molnár admired his boss, József Vészi, perhaps the most influential editor in the country. Vészi liked to invite handsome, brilliant young intellectuals to his frequent parties. He had four highly cultured daughters. It did not take Molnár too long to select the sixteen-year-old Margit, who had a devilish, challenging look in her eyes. She was beautiful and gifted, and attracted attention as both a writer and an artist. Margit had an army of admirers, too, but no one could compete with Molnár. He was not in a hurry in his courtship and she was very patient for the impulsive and spoiled person she was. It took six years for Molnár to take the plunge. The marriage of Molnár to Margit Vészi was a great social event in 1906. Their daughter, Márta, was born the following year, but by that time the "fabulous" marriage was already disintegrating. Molnár was not the ideal husband, nor Margit the ideal wife. Both of them were stars, and since there could be only one star for either of them, the incompatibility was obvious. The verbal fights increased in intensity and—we are told—so did the physical ones. The separation was as quick as the courtship had been long.[10]

Molnár's brooding over the marital shipwreck, however, was not prolonged. Within a few months he was seriously involved with Hungary's leading actress, Irén Varsányi, wife of a wealthy manufacturer, Illés Szécsi. It is for Irén that Molnár wrote *Az ördög* (The Devil), wherein he challenged the actress to leave

her prosaic husband. The play, performed in 1907, brought
Molnár international fame, membership in the exclusive Petőfi
Society, and a two-week jail sentence, following the much-
publicized duel with the jealous Szécsi. In the same year Molnár
wrote three books, among them the outstanding juvenile novel
A Pál-utcai Fiúk (The Paul Street Boys). Soon after his father's
death, in 1908, he finished his best short story collection, entitled
Muzsika (Music). However, his fame reached its height with
the successful performances of *Liliom* abroad, though the play
initially had been a failure in Budapest. Eventually it became
his best-known play. The gossip-hungry Budapest populace
stormed the theaters to watch the new developments in the playwright's private life, since these autobiographical plays often
disclosed the latest details of Molnár's complicated lovelife.
"Having sought to propitiate his angry wife in *Liliom* by portraying her in the unforgettable role of Juli, Molnár then proceeded in *The Guardsman* and in *The Wolf* to reveal and explain
the complexity of his affair with Irén Varsányi."[11] Budapest
reveled in discussing the liaison between the celebrated actress
and her equally famous beau. When, however, the lovers made
arrangements for moving in together, Varsányi's young daughter
suddenly became seriously ill. Overcome by guilt, the mother
returned to her family and abruptly terminated the affair. The
abandoned playwright, not accustomed to rejection, fell into
deep depression, started to drink heavily, and even tried to
commit suicide.[12]

During his recovery Molnár continued writing: he was slowly
becoming a legend. His prolificacy was phenomenal. From 1910
until 1914, five Molnár volumes of collected essays and feuilletons were published, in addition to his translations of over
thirty French plays—primarily the comedies of Robert de Flers,
Armande Caillavet, and Pierre de Marivaux.[13]

The first year of World War I found Molnár traveling over
the devastated battlefields with the Austro-Hungarian forces. He
was sent there as a reporter by his friend Andor Miklós, editor
of *Az Est* (The Evening), a popular daily he and Molnár had
founded in 1910.[14] His vivid accounts of the war demonstrated
once more his remarkable journalistic talent. These reports were
published regularly also in the *London Morning Post* and the

New York Times, and were collected eventually in two volumes: *Egy haditudósitó emlékei* (A War Correspondent's Diary). Molnár's distinguished service at the front was rewarded by the Emperor, who conferred the "Franz Joseph Order" on him. The performance of his new play, *A fehér felhő* (The White Cloud), written at army headquarters, won him the Voinits Avard, Hungary's "Tony," and membership in the Kisfaludy Society, an exclusive literary association. In 1917, he wrote several plays, among them *Farsang* (Carnival), *Úridivat* (Fashions for Men), and two volumes of humoresques. In addition, he started a major novel, *Andor*, which was published the following year. During and after the revolution of 1918, Molnár kept on working feverishly as a journalist but characteristically avoided political involvement.

Molnár's first postwar play, *A hattyú* (The Swan), a beguiling satire of royalty and the absurdities of the vanishing court life, was produced in 1920. In the same year it ran successfully on every major European stage. With the profits of *The Swan* assured, Molnár was able to turn to experimentation with new dramatic techniques. In the ensuing four years he wrote six plays in rapid succession.[15] His personal life was no less dazzling: a ten-year-long stormy love affair with Hungary's tempestuous prima donna Sári Fedák finally culminated in a much-noted wedding in 1922.

Again two stars united and both tried to outshine the other; neither of them wanted to yield. The gossip columnists of the papers were kept busy reporting the verbal and fist fights in the Molnár household. Hauntingly reminiscent of his first marriage, the nuptials marked the end, rather than the beginning, of their relationship. While the public still gloated over his turbulent life, the literary elite shunned him and openly began attacking their former favorite.

By the 1920s Molnár was acclaimed internationally as one of the most gifted contemporary dramatists, but in Hungary he had to pay a penalty for his long and undisputed dominance of the stage. His café entourage began to dwindle and the local critics no longer praised him indiscriminately. In fact, some of them viewed him with outright malice. After 1920 Molnár spent less and less time in Budapest. The Budapest literary circles' resentment over this "defection" was compounded by his main offence: he was a "commercial" success. To become wealthy out of literature was considered vulgar enough, but to collect thousands of dollars from the United States was the ultimate aberration. Malicious colleagues referred to him as "Checkspeare" and the Molnár boycott spread. The disenchanted playwright pretended to ignore his critics but his absences from his native city kept getting longer. In the following two decades Molnár became "a denizen of the world."

III   The Wanderer

Between 1920 and 1930 Molnár's income was impressive—over $1 million—so that he could afford the maintenance of what he called his "five-room apartment," accommodations with staff in the finest hotels of Budapest, Vienna, Karsbald, Venice, and Nice. Visiting his homes, Molnár traveled frequently and in style.

When he married the actress Sári Fedák, he was already involved emotionally with another actress, Lili Darvas, a sixteen-year-old stage star of Budapest. In *Launzi* Darvas played the lead so well that Molnár created *The Red Mill* and *The Glass Slipper* exclusively for her. The incensed Fedák reacted at once: for revenge, she asked Melchior Lengyel, another noted Hungarian playwright, to write a play specifically for her. To this public humiliation Molnár retorted by divorcing Fedák in 1924.[16]

Scandals and legal entanglements enmeshed the master of comedies, so in 1925 he moved to Vienna. A few months later Molnár married Lili Darvas, who had recently become a member of the Max Reinhardt Theatre Company. For a while he accompanied his wife on her tours: the newlyweds were much on the road since the company rotated among the theaters of Berlin, Vienna, and Salzburg. In 1926 Molnár presented his wife with *Játék a kastélyban* (The Play's the Thing) and *Riviera*. The former play temporarily reinstated Budapest's prodigal son into the good graces of his native city. Even his most inveterate enemies were silenced by the brilliance and success of this suavely cynical, highly amusing caprice. It ran in all major European theaters, and opened on Broadway the same year.

Rewards were heaped upon him. In 1927, after the Paris premiere of *The Swan*, Molnár was decorated with the cross of the Legion of Honor; then he received a hero's welcome in America. After his arrival in New York, theater directors and publishers besieged the couple with offers and invitations. They were received by President Coolidge in the White House, and Molnár's fiftieth birthday was celebrated with much fanfare on Broadway. Before leaving, the author accepted the offer of joining the contributors' staff of *Vanity Fair*.

After their return to Budapest in 1928, Molnár wrote a new play, *Olympia*, and a volume of sketches. He supervised the publication of his *Collected Works* in Hungarian, which was followed by an English edition, released in New York in 1929. While zig-zagging across Europe, toasting with kings and presidents, partying with stage dignitaries, and gambling in casinos on the Riviera, Molnár found time to write a play a year between 1929 and 1932.[17] As her husband basked in the limelight, Darvas, a world-famous star by now, traveled extensively. The lengthy separations affected their relationship. The middle-aged Molnár wanted a permanent partner, someone always at hand to cater to his emotional and physical needs. Darvas could not fulfill this role. Thus, they parted amicably, remaining married and friends till his death. In 1932 Molnár met Wanda Bartha, a young, cultured Hungarian divorcée who joined the playwright as a secretary and companion and remained with him for the rest of her life.

In the 1930s Molnár, with his keen insight, felt that a debacle was approaching. He moved from one country to another, always on the go. In those days, the one-time raconteur and "free spirit" found consolation in Bible study. This led to his writing a religious drama, *Csoda a hegyek között* (Miracle in the Mountain), centering around Jesus, and a new novel *Zenélő angyal* (Angel making Music), both published in 1933. The following year he turned to lighter themes again in *Az ismeretlen lány* (Girl from Triest or The Unknown Girl) and in *Nagy szerelem* (Great Love). Molnár's ability to transform any kind of personal experience into an effective work of art began to shrivel. His frequent anxieties and mild depressions, mingled with painful nostalgia for his youth and former glory, were reflected in several comparatively weak plays and novels, A zöld huszár (The Green Hussar) and Őszi utazás (Autumn Journey), published in 1937 and 1939.

In 1937, Molnár attended the opening of his latest play, Delila (Blue Danube), the last of the many effervescent and noisy Budapest premieres, and in September left the capital for the last time. He never saw his native city again. Although Wanda and Molnár still lived in unperturbed luxury, staying mostly in Venice, the growing threat of Fascism and the pressing political and economic problems convinced Molnár that his days were numbered on the Continent. In those years he lived like a recluse. The events had unhinged his optimism: times were grim, and the easy mechanics of levity served him no more; the scope for comedy had shrunk because the world was on the verge of tragedy.

1939, the outbreak of World War II, found him in Switzerland ready to say farewell to Europe. On December 31, he left Geneva and sailed for New York. He arrived on January 12, 1940, his sixty-second birthday, and was welcomed by Lili Darvas, who was still his wife officially, by Gilbert Miller, and by some of his Hungarian friends. A room was reserved for him in the Plaza Hotel, and Molnár moved into Room 835, his last abode; the new immigrant stayed there until his death.

IV   The Émigré

It was no easy task for the aging author, who spoke no English, to adjust to the New World, but the hectic tempo of New York and the novelty of his adopted country had a rejuvenating effect on him. Soon after his arrival, he was busy at his desk and finished a comedy, A cukrászné (Delicate Story), reminiscent of the light farces of yore. It opened on Broadway in December 1940. With the help of his devoted secretary, Wanda, who had joined him in May, Molnár proceeded to rewrite and polish his earlier works, studied English, and occasionally entertained members of the émigré colony.

Yielding to tempting offers from Hollywood, Molnár visited the movie capital in 1941 and came back flooded by new ideas and contract promises. His new play, *A király szolgálólánya* (The King's Maid) a pathos-ridden religious tragedy, was a failure. But the temporary setback stimulated rather than discouraged the author. With feverish speed, in less than two years, he completed a sentimental juvenile story, *Kékszemű* (The Blue-Eyed Lady), and three plays, *A császár* (The Emperor), two versions of *Panoptikum* (Waxworks) and . . . *Or Not To Be.* The last one has never been translated into Hungarian. He wrote these works in Hungarian, then translated them into rough English, which Mrs. Bartha and his friends polished for the official version. After 1941 all the final versions of Molnár's manuscripts submitted to his agents were written in English mostly by himself.

The alarming news about the atrocities and horrors of the war seriously disturbed Molnár. In 1943 he suffered a massive heart attack which incapacitated him for a long time: the industrious playwright had to rest and suspend work for almost a year. Molnár celebrated the end of World War II with the publication of a new novel, *Isten veled szivem* (Farewell My Heart), and the English edition of *The Captain of St. Margaret's*, a revised, expanded version of an early short story, "The Steam Pillar." It was at this time that the author gradually learned the tragic fate of hundreds of his Jewish friends and associates. Understandably, Molnár reacted with strong emotions: he was outraged and depressed; his personality underwent a transformation. He became apathetic, morose, a misanthrope. In 1946, he received with indifferent resignation the news about the Budapest opening of *The Emperor*. But the worst was yet to come.

The following year, Molnár experienced his first major tragedy: Wanda Bartha took her life. It is not known why this devoted, loving companion resorted to this decision. Guesses are many: perhaps she brooded over the loss of her family, particularly a favorite brother murdered by the Nazis; perhaps the demoralizing, often cruel attitude of the changed Molnár had gradually undermined her mental equilibrium. Her suicide devastated Molnár; for weeks he was in a state of shock and he never really recovered from the loss. "Wanda died—my one light went out—on August 27 or 28, in New York. . . . There is no more hope in life! Wanda made the idea of my death, which had always filled

me with horror, endurable for me."[18] Determined to pay a lasting tribute to her memory, the deeply shaken, unconsolable
writer started his most tragic work, *Companion in Exile*, a com-
pilation of autobiographical notes, recalling the dedicated friend's
sacrifices, reminiscing about the happy times they had spent
together. He also included the daily logs Wanda had kept for
years, supervising its English translation word by word. The
publication of the book brought no comfort: it was received with
polite indifference. Soon after her death, Molnár bequeathed all
his manuscripts and volumes of bound scrapbooks—containing
clippings and articles about him, prepared by Wanda—to the
New York Public Library, "in the memory of his beloved friend
and literary advisor." The celebrated entertainer, the self-
confident social lion, became a broken man, subject to crying
spells. He bitterly complained about his bereavement to his wife,
Miss Darvas, one of the few people he was willing to face occasionally: "the inconsiderateness of her! How dared she, oh, how
could she abandon me?"[19]

With self-discipline, Molnár tried seeking solace in hard work,
laboring for the sake of labor, not because of any need for
recognition or success. "There is only one consolation on earth
and that is work," he used to say. He adhered to his thesis most
strenuously. This total absorption in work was also an obvious
effort to reaffirm and prolong the self-deception that he would
not die. While these late works continued to display his sparkling
technique, they often sounded hollow, like faded echoes of
the past. Molnár's plays were still running in many theaters;
movie and television adapations were made of some of them,
and new editions of his works were planned.[20] Yet, he seemed
unconcerned and rarely left his hotel room as the years passed.
Visitors who made attempts to cheer him up could meet the
former gourmand patronizing a simple restaurant on 58th Street.
Even those who were permitted by Molnár to sit down with him
stayed briefly because of his angry moods or pathetic crying
fits. So, people came less and less often.

Even though Molnár's health was failing, he went on writing
until his collapse. The race against death was as arduous as it
was self-destructive. On March 22, he had a seizure and, after
an unsuccessful operation, he died of stomach cancer, at Mt.

Sinai Hospital, April 1, 1952. Obituaries around the world paid tribute to his creative genius. "Immersed in the memory of Budapest's golden days, the Hungarian Molière, as he was often called, sought but never found here an equivalent for the city of his youth."[21] He was buried with the ministrations of a rabbi in Linden Hill Cemetery, next to Wanda Bartha. The Hungarian cosmopolitan died in exile as an American. Because of his superstitious fear that in preparing a will he would hasten his death, Molnár died intestate, leaving several manuscripts and unfinished work and a great deal of money behind. In sad contrast to his colorful life, the funeral was very quiet, attended only by his wife and a few friends; doubtless he was also mourned by his daughter and three grandchildren in Budapest—perhaps even by his two ex-wives—and perhaps by not a few surviving admirers around the world. As S. N. Behrman stated, "He had the poise of a man, who, in spite of wars, persecutions, and imperious personal drives, among them the almost searing dualism of the impulse to suffer and the impulse to impose suffering, had yet managed to make his life, on the whole, pretty much what he wanted it."[22]

In the name of all women Molnár had loved, Lili Darvas bid him farewell with a quotation: "Liliom, sleep my boy, sleep!"

CHAPTER 3

Molnár the Storyteller: From Editorials to Short Stories

I The Journalist

MOLNÁR always considered himself a journalist and he achieved high distinction both in the Hungarian and the international press. As a chronicler of Budapest, he left an indelible mark on Hungarian short prose. Nevertheless, only half-hearted attention was given to him as a journalist after he had become a celebrated playwright.

In the 1890s, when he embarked on his journalistic career as a volunteer at Vészi's *Budapesti Napló*, there was no distinct demarcation between journalism and what is now loosely called "creative work." Most of the poets, novelists, and playwrights wrote for daily papers or periodicals; journalism was their mainstay. None of them deemed this labor inferior to his personal, imaginative work. After all, newspapers disseminated all types of literature and reached the largest reading public. Molnár's definition of the Hungarian newspapermen's role at that time reveals his pride in the profession.

Reporters in America and elsewhere go out and get the news, whereas we, more often than not stay in the office or in our garrets and make the "news." By that I mean that we report the news of the mind and soul of our characters as much as we do the actions and happenings of daily life, which are, after all, the material accidents of existence rather than the significant realities of life. There is a disposition in some quarters to call all that fiction. But some of it, I insist, is literature. True literature is life translated into letters.[1]

There were other reasons for the leading authors' close association with newspaper work. Budapest was developing at a hectic pace and few people had time to read novels. The ones who bought books preferred foreign works; quoting from Zola or Wilde was considered "sophisticated." Molnár himself pointed out: "for years essays or short stories remained the only literary genre a writer could hope to sell because people were reluctant to read Hungarian novels, except Jókai's. Consequently, all of us were compelled to write short prose, often squandering our best ideas by reducing them to the limited length of newspaper stories and feuilletons. . . . Since we had been confined to this genre, it miraculously ascended to the highest level in the world."[2] Furthermore, the task of giving high quality native literature, however brief, to a fast growing public was a source of challenge and joy for ambitious young authors. As journalists, they could shape the language and coin new words that expressed the new ideas and the complicated internal revolution of modern urban man. The burgeoning journals provided an excellent forum for experimentation; young Molnár, ardent to mold language and people alike, quickly seized this opportunity and swore his allegiance to the papers.

In those days, dailies had no separate sections or specialized staff to cover foreign news, finance, theater, sports, and music. Reporters had to be versatile: they were expected to gain expertise in all spheres of activity. At first, cashing in on his legal background, Molnár worked as a court reporter, but soon he expanded his scope. His caustic editorials and humorous short sketches in the manner of the French wit of Alfred Capus, Henri Bernstein, and Tristan Bernard soon attracted attention.[3]

At the *Budapesti Napló* the young novice was welcomed by his colleagues, among them such notables as Sándor Bródy, Zoltán Ambrus, Dániel Papp, and Zoltán Thury, "veterans" of the feuilleton genre. They had been well-known chroniclers of Budapest who consistently strove to portray social injustice and the exigencies of the poor just as accurately as the psychological anguish of the bourgeoisie. Molnár's apprenticeship was not arduous: he learned the skills and grasped the mechanics in a short time, and with amazing self-confidence and productivity, at once produced meticulously structured, ingenious articles. He rose to eminence as a "city columnist," an interpreter and critic of the peculiar temper of the Budapest middle class. His writings blended a unique sarcasm, a touch of sentimentality, and a large dose of cynicism—the accepted "Gallic" note of the metropolitan spirit. This spirit emanated from the cafés, which were, according to Molnár, the "real offices" of the Hungarian men of letters: "We did our writing in those places not to be Bohemian but because most of us did not have any other decent quarters."[4] Of course Molnár always had a home, but he wanted to be "where the action was."

Molnár gradually transcended the qualities of his models and discarded the influence of his mentors. This overconfident individualism understandably alienated some of his colleagues, and it did not take him long to realize that talent and self-assurance produced powerful enemies. At the *Napló*, Sándor Bródy was his mentor and closest friend at first; the renowned author "adopted" the young Molnár and introduced him into literary circles, taught him the craft, entertained him in his home, and made him a permanent "club member" in his café.[5] But even the critics admitted that no one could really be considered Molnár's literary tutor; he created a new satirical tone, an ironic, anecdotal style, and in his sketches a unique technique of dramatic dialogue which became Molnár's characteristic manner of expression.

II *Sketches, Satires, Feuilletons*

Molnár's essays and dialogues were collected in several volumes over the years: *Józsi és egyéb kis komédiák* (Józsi and Other Small Comedies), 1902; *Pesti Erkölcsök* (Metropolitan Morals), 1904; *Hétágú Síp* (Pipes of Pan), 1911; *Ma, tegnap, tegnapelőtt* (Today, Yesterday, Tomorrow), 1912; *Az Aruvimi erdő titka és egyéb szatirák* (The Secret of the Aruwim Forest and Other Satires), 1917; *Ismerősök* (Acquaintances), 1917; and *Toll* (Pen), 1928. These books, comprised of anecdotes, yarns, skits, satires, jokes, epigrams, chronicles, impressions, formal editorials, dialogues and odd types, reveal a wide spectrum of Molnár's contribution to journalism. Dozens of these stories and dialogues appeared in various editions under different titles with minor variations. The author defined these collections as "combinations of a diary and newspaper articles, a sort of hybrid genre; initially they had been written as diaries but their writer knew that as soon as the ink dried on the pages, the printer's ink would wet them again."[6] Many of these sketches and dialogues were published in American magazines and twenty selections were compiled in a volume entitled *Husbands and Lovers*, but only *Stories for Two* was translated into English in its entirety.

In *Józsi* and *Children* Molnár sensitively probed into children's psyche. Instead of adorning youth with a halo, he dissected the juvenile soul with keen perception and uncanny knowledge. The portrayal of young people's pranks, exuberance, nobility, and folly was full of humor and gentle compassions. In *Józsi* the protagonist is a pampered, obnoxious child who disrupts, terrorizes, and tyrannizes his adult environment, a typical Budapest *enfant terrible* for whom a good joke is worth everything even if others get hurt. Contemporaries seemed to hear unmistakable autobiographical echoes in the hilarity of Józsi; one of them, B. Halmi, observed, "It is my firm conviction that in *Józsi* the author presented his own calling card; his fictional teaser *Pester Kind*, that ruthless and grotesque creature, imbued with Jewish humor, mockery, puns and conceit, is none other than the miniature Molnár."[7] His sister, Erzsébet, substantiates this in her book, *Testvérek voltunk* (We were Siblings). Józsi cheats, lies, blackmails, imitating freely all he sees his parents are doing in a more subtle manner. "The most cruel humans are children," Molnár remarked once. Other dialogues introduce children in different dramatic encounters: a dying six-year-old boy discusses death with his playmate ("Horse's Feather"); two little girls chatter about the sycophant nature of adults as they are being scrubbed to be presentable before a visiting countess ("Two Little Angels"). In "First Step" a teenage girl acts like a miniature of the "Molnáresque woman," displaying a penchant for elusive impishness. She lies glibly and easily outwits the unsuspecting boyfriend. The volume's short, sparkling persiflages, adorned with astute punchlines, are authentic presentations of not only children's attitudes but also the capital's atmosphere.

Molnár indeed penetrates children's mentality; he knows intimately their confused, naive world, the pains of growing up, as well as their language at various ages. These early portraits foreshadow the "child psychologist" Molnár of *The Derelict Boat*

and *The Paul Street Boys*. One of his colleagues, Dezső Kosztolányi, who was also intrigued by children and described them in
his novels, tried to explain Molnár's exceptionally keen interest
in children in this way: "To me Molnár will always remain the
most sensitive poet of children's psyche. . . . His wide-eyed, inexperienced, pure creatures—obvious candidates of heaven—in truth
concealed terrifying internal hell. Why did he love children so
much then? Because to him they were potential devils: the
writer's favorite dramatic personas."[8] Friends were wary of Molnár's unequivocal sincerity concerning children. This child expert
in fiction cared little about his own daughter, whom he hardly
met, nor did he help his own grandchildren; also he was reputed
to be visibly irritated by his friends' offsprings when they appeared in his company.

In *Metropolitan Morals* Molnár dwells upon his favorite
themes: fraud, avarice, mendacity, corruption, snobbery, sneaky
revenge, and other mischiefs—in short, the immorality of Budapest. With witty sarcasm, the twenty-five-year-old journalist
playfully spins stories of universal types and human foibles depicting how people behave at a barbershop, at the zoo while
watching an exotic animal, on the skating-rink for the first time,
or at a photographer's studio. In "The Shoehorn" he presents a
novice salesman who gets away with bringing out the same
shoe each time customers request to try on another pair. In
"Inflation" a man enumerates his silly expenditures then turns
around and irately refuses to raise the servant's wage even by
a few pennies. Molnár's pen is dipped in diluted gall when he
attacks the parsimony of the Jewish bourgeoisie and the social
and cultural snobbery of the *nouveau riche*.

In *Stories for Two*, a collection of humorous dialogues primarily
dealing with people in love, the pungency and perfect timing
portend Molnár's skill as a playwright. In fact, some of these
scenes appeared in *Husbands and Lovers* and were later elaborated into full-length plays.[9] Here Molnár's bittersweet comments or verbal pondering on infidelity and female fickleness,
as well as his presentation of melòdramatic encounters of lovelorn people, add up to more than a self-conscious *tour de force*.
In these impressionistic sketches, the interplay between illusion
and reality is a major vehicle of conveying his message; illusion

is truth simply because people believe it. There is no saying where reality, that elusive if not nonexistent thing, may lie hidden. Hence, Molnár created a world of pretense where stolen handkerchiefs are ostentatiously kept near a man's heart in hope of gaining favors by such silly displays; where "the most unpardonable sin a woman can commit is telling the truth." It is a world where the heart of a mother breaks as she falls in love with a phantom idol described in her daughter's diary; where flirtatious middle-aged women ruthlessly chaff one young admirer only to entice another; where "the institution of marriage seems bankrupt and obsolete"; where passions prevail, where ladies sigh as they sum up their philosophy: "To preserve an illusion a woman lives on lies and defends herself with lies . . ." ("Railway Accident"). While the plots are somewhat slight and one-dimensional and the characterization seems too deliberate sometimes, the volume contains some of Molnár's wittiest dialogues. Best known is "Alfred, Dear" (also known as "The Witch"), a one-act play often performed together with some of his relatively shorter plays. In this playlet, a cunning actress placates a hysterical, jealous wife while the husband is hiding in the closet. Steeped in cynicism, the protagonist epitomizes all crafty women in Molnár's field of vision.

To further support his thesis on feminine inconsistency and the demoralizing effect of money, Molnár again aims at his pet targets: devious women, self-assertive snobs, and Jewish parvenues in *Pipes of Pan*. Especially witty are those sarcastic sketches in which women are pitted against phoney upstarts, quacks, and journalists of the scandal sheets. The volume's eight-part feature story, "Pig Slaughter in the Leopold District," is an acerbic social satire on the pretentious braggadocio of the new rich. A pompous Jewish banker reenacts a country-style pig-slaughtering ceremony in his plush city apartment, starring an enormous Yorkshire sow, temporarily stowed away in the bathtub. Molnár's burlesque humor here is particularly scintillating in his tendential understatements and bent for the unexpected.

Molnár's Sunday editorials for the *Pesti Hirlap*, collected in *Today, Yesterday, Tomorrow*, reveal once more his journalistic talent. The chronicler ponders suicides and their causes, new inventions and their effect, cafés and casinos and their social functions, the despair of municipal employees, or the Magyar image riddled with Balkan flaws. After an anecdotal start, he plunges into serious discussions substantiating his thesis with convincing evidence, proving his point clearly and amusingly. The denounement is often a scathing indictment of Hungary's social ills and an eloquent cry for humanism.

Molnár's tone sharpens to thorny satire in *The Secret of the Aruwim Forest and Other Stories*. The themes of these essays, written during World War I, are reflective of both the author's and the country's anguish. Molnár scourges Hungary's conservatism, the people's overzealous, servile adoration of foreigners, and the still-prevailing provincial attitude in the capital. He also scorns aggressive charity drives, blood-sucking lawyers and tax-collectors, and the hypocritical "champions of truth." One terse feuilleton, "Scientific Thirst," deals with Budapest's pseudo-scientific approach to sex, and discusses how blatantly people distorted Freud's teachings.

The title story is a highly stylized, acerbic social satire written in a style anticipating Art Buchwald. The protagonist, Mr. Honest, an impoverished clerk and father of nineteen children, tries to refuse bribe money and is getting ready to unveil a horrendous corruption scheme he accidentally discovered. Big businessmen and politicians, whose interests are in jeopardy, trick their indignant "critic" into entering the Aruwim "Horror Factory." With the fantasy of an Expressionistic science-fiction writer, Molnár describes the place in great detail. It is a gigantic arena full of complicated electrical gadgets and strange, perpetually moving machines, "torture trees," designed to transform people into obedient robots. When a victim gets through, if he ever does, he will never question anything but will "play the game as everyone does." This automated "forest"—a modern version of Dante's Hell—seems impenetrable at first, but Mr. Honest finally winds his way through. When he wakes up—it all turns out to be a nightmare—he rejects the Judas money and swears to continue his struggle for decency. The moral is spelled out in the title: people of integrity must learn the lesson, "the secret" of the Aruwim Forest. Six years later he expanded this story into a fantasy play, *The Red Mill*, which met the same controversial reception as the original tale.

Molnár's tone is more subdued in his other volume published in the same year. *Acquaintances* is a collection of sensitive character portraits encompassing metropolitan stereotypes. A familiar array of policemen, paper vendors, waiters, coachmen and journalists are sketched here in pastel hues. The story of a twelve-year-old bellboy who works thirteen hours a day and travels five to help his widowed mother is a heart-warming tear-jerker ("Lencsés"). The volume contains a few sophisticated book reviews and also a long treatise on Hungarian journalism, "Decameron."

The taunting critical tone and numerous references to social inadequacies notwithstanding, *Pen,* another colorful kaleidoscope of Budapest's typical figures, contains only variations on Molnár's old themes.[10] The volume's brief, perceptive diary entries are an adroit matrix of mild attacks at avarice, vanity, prejudice and other human foibles. It is also a series of witty love-letters addressed to Budapest, his "village of birth," his "mother city," each adorned with the author's sentimental or/and cynical stamp. In Communist Hungary, even the staunchest critics, who consistently disparaged his accomplishments, acknowledge Molnár's merits as a fine local colorist. One of these scholars, Irén Vécsei, views Molnár as: "an unfailing lover of Budapest, so overwhelmed by his city that he could pay attention to little else. Still, we must record his newspaper work as the best of Hungary's journalistic legacy. His articles, for the first time, captured and simultaneously judged a unique era, its flavor and its life-style."[11]

Molnár's journalistic output was rich and versatile. His clever, meticulously constructed articles were written in clear, simple style. A born reporter, Molnár was perceptive, courageous, accurate, and always interesting. He found sensitive nerves and wittily exposed social and human abuses. In apparent contradiction, however, he never made any attempt to analyze causes or offer remedies.

For three decades Molnár worked assiduously as a reporter. Why did he pursue this profession? For money? He was rich. For fame? He had been world renowned as a playwright since 1908. To transmit his dialectic messages to the readers? Perhaps. But he had shunned "Messianic" revolutionaries all his life. Why, then? Molnár always did what he liked, and he apparently loved this genre; the press provided yet another outlet for him to entertain and please people. That is why his reportage, though written with élan, talent, and professionalism, never delved too deeply and never pricked the reader's conscience. His facile stories touched only the surface, merely exposing problems but never probing into their roots. Though Molnár was not averse to criticizing the Establishment, he maintained that thorough-going social criticism was not the writer's but the social scientist's task. For this seeming lack of social consciousness he has been repeatedly condemned by critics. Nevertheless, his accomplishment in the field of journalism was impressive enough to deserve literary recognition.

III   *The War Correspondent*

The outbreak of World War I did not stir strong emotions in Molnár; he viewed wars as natural phenomena and made no attempt to analyze their historical, economic, or social causes. Despite his "apolitical" attitude, his war diaries enhanced his reputation as one of the best reporters of his time. He was recognized by dozens of leading papers in England and in the USA which regularly published his coverage, even though Hungary belonged to the opposing camp. Molnár spent over a year on the front with the Austro-Hungarian forces, collecting news, recording impressions, roaming about ditches and among ramshackle houses and burnt-out villages. At this time the reporter's customary cynicism vanished: his vivid daily chronicles, filled with warmth, pathos, and humor, realistically captured the atmosphere in the dramas of life and death, and brought them shockingly close to the readers. One of his reports was a detailed account of the Przemysl retreat and its catastrophic result. It began with Molnár's impressions recorded shortly before the massive enemy attack was launched: "The Russian artillery was on the hill opposite our lines. While I was in the trenches, they sent over only four shrapnels. However, these were not the well-known 'war-correspondent's shells' which land barely ten feet from the writer. They were angry shots, but they burst more than thousand feet from where we stood. . . . By the way, to stand for long hours in putrid, filthy dugouts, in freezing water or in melting snow, even if there were no other danger of life in war, would be the most supreme of all human sacrifices. . . ."[12]

Maintaining his high style, Molnár neither glorified the war nor exaggerated patriotic sentimentality. Without passing judgment, he simply transmitted events and people's reactions to countless horrors from a human point of view, portraying soldiers and civilians as tragic victims of a senseless bloodbath and needless destruction.

A deft reporter, Molnár seemed to be present everywhere; he conducted interviews with fighters of all ranks, and POWs; he copied leaflets, military orders, war songs, letters written by ordinary infantrymen, and heart-rending replies from home. Sometimes he enclosed little maps and meticulous sketches of the troops' positions in certain battles. In addition to making affectionate comments on the sacrifices and heroism of the fighters, the diaries also recorded their fears, petty quarrels over barrack chores, and gathered scores of rowdy army jokes.

In 1916, these articles were published in two volumes, entitled, *Diary of a War Correspondent, 1914–1915*. In the introduction Molnár wrote: "This is neither a diary nor the history of the war; it's only a record of the agonizing memories of a war correspondent's one year at the front, a chronicle of events and people, little and big, important and seemingly insignificant." The book forms a document of real importance. It is a tender epitaph of the supreme heroism of the nameless thousands, especially of the Hungarian Hussars and infantrymen. The *Diary* bears Molnár's deep humanity: neither articulating empty patriotic sentiments nor damning the enemy, he only advocates his motto: "Live and Let Live!"

IV Short Stories

Of the twenty volumes of his *Collected Works*, published in 1928, Molnár designated only two collections as short stories: *Muzsika* (Music, 1908) and *Kis hármaskönyv* (Three in One, 1914). Some of these stories had previously been published in newspapers and included in other volumes; some served as drafts for plays ("Bedtime Story" is *Liliom*'s outline), and novels ("The

Steampillar" is the basis of *The Captain of St. Margaret's*). After a brief general observation about the stories, a few outstanding ones from both collections will be discussed here in detail.

Both volumes deal primarily with urban people: bankers, artisans, Bohemians, and women of all types, from princess to prostitute. The tone is again anecdotal, satirical, and the dramatic dialogue is the main form of expression. The writer shows remarkable narrative ability in his realistic characterization and in his manner of controlling the plot with unerring technique and with the logic of a *routinier*. As critic J. Remenyi observes, "Molnár could give body even to seemingly unimportant or temporary ideas and whims; . . . he was an expert of carefully studied simplicities that he turned into universal complexities."[13]

The form of delivery varies: confessions written in letter form; extended anecdotes; formal novellas with dramatic dialogues; some embody momentary emotions or whims, and others elaborate on background and personality development. Molnár is always a meticulous writer but in his *bona fide* short stories he seems to use more symbolic language and more poetic devices than in his feuilletons. Regrettably not one of these stories has appeared in English: only one later story, written in 1926, "Gőzoszlop" (Steam Pillar), was translated as part of a novel.[14]

The short stories' style reflects Molnár's dazzling playwriting skills; to delineate both characters and atmosphere authentically, he often uses the colloquial talk of the Budapest salons and streets. He writes in a clear style, using a dramatically intense and concise vocabulary which is interspersed with picturesque phrases and whimsical symbols and is embellished with irony. He quickly establishes contact with the readers by addressing them directly, and is capable of making the fantastic seem real, the insignificant horrendous, the artificial natural, without becoming overly complex.[15]

Like the dialogues, the short stories also feature women as chief protagonists. These sensual and powerful females make men prisoners of their desires, keeping them in perpetual excitement by fomenting their jealousy. Women provide both sexual ecstasy and reasons for doubt. Generally, man suffers on account of a woman but a woman seldom suffers because of a man. In the game of sexes, the gallant, insecure men observe the rules, but women do not; they sadistically enjoy trampling upon their partners' pride and dignity. In both his plays and stories jealousy is one of Molnár's paramount subjects.

The other frequent topic is the portrayal of the suffering of the poor and the losers. A cavalcade of servants, derelicts, street-walkers, starving artists, orphans, and beggars is shown with compassion and understanding. Molnár keeps balance by his sense of proportion and his naturalistic description of the setting.

Molnár's first short-story collection, *Music*, contained eighteen diverse tales of varying length. The contemporary critic Miksa Fenyő considered it important because this volume of short prose, he claims, included the author's best novellas, which "exude lovable witticism, light and facile wisdom . . . instead of placing foul ideals on the pillory, Molnár exposes life's physical flaws: its blisters, freckles, chewed-up nails and baldness."[16]

"Coal Pilferers," Molnár's finest naturalistic tale, is a poetic, well-constructed, sardonic story about three starving, sooty men hired to transport coal for a wealthy dealer. One misty October morning they decide to steal some coal by tossing the bigger lumps into the bushes as they drive the loaded wagon. On their way back they plan to gather them up. Exhilarated by the prospect of warm rooms or a bit of extra money, the pilferers joyfully keep throwing down the "black diamonds" from the cart. Soon, a similarly poor red-cap and his assistant, pulling a go-cart bearing heavy luggage and its owner, a shriveled old lady, discover the scattered coal. They come across two policemen, one an impoverished father of six, the other a tuberculous, weak man barely able to breathe. The porter reports the strange "findings" to them. Just then, the excited group is joined by a shabby wharf-guard announcing that he, too, has found some coal. Initially, each of these miserable creatures, prospective thieves themselves, is tempted to become an accessory, but drilled-in honesty over-comes greed. Posing as outraged "law abiding" citizens, they agree to denounce the thieves who arrive at the scene at the crucial moment. Paupers judging paupers, the woebegone informers gloat over the bad luck of their "comrades"; in trying to impress one another, the "coppers" view the "robbers" with disdain. As the group silently turns toward the police precinct, the old woman makes a futile attempt of protest, but no one hears her feeble voice.

The psychological motivation of each character is used as an artistic vehicle to develop the plot. With sharp irony, Molnár states his message at the end: "They marched forward—all of them poor and miserable, chronically ill because of unhealthy abodes, victims of horrifying, suffocating, murderous poverty; a small ragged army of decrepit, pale, starving men except for the red-cap. He was rich: recently he could afford meat almost every day! . . . On this lulling, luke-warm October day, little people sent each other to prison for a few lumps of coal—all could have been defendants, plaintiffs, witnesses, informers, and thieves-of-thieves; not one of them was right, yet all were right . . . wretched, hungry, shivering, sick victims. . . ."[17] The poetic description of nature's glory provides a sharp contrast to the hopeless misery of the realistically sketched characters. Molnár's artistic juxtaposition of naturalistic setting and characters reminds us of the opening paragraphs of Steinbeck's *Of Mice and Men*.

The title story, "Music," occupies a unique position among the volume's novellas because of its highly symbolic style. The theme, the intangible power of music, is also rather atypical of Molnár. The plot centers around a poor, bright, tubercular school teacher who was jilted by his rich, dull, healthy fiancée. She chooses a robust, vigorous lad in his stead. On the day before the wedding, the heartbroken lover goes to the church to practice at the organ. Totally enraptured by the magic of sounds, he produces such heavenly melodies that baffle even himself. A little later he sees the bride enter; she is promptly bewitched by the music. Elated, he bids her farewell through the ether: "First it was the virgin knight of the Holy Grail who kept singing to his princess . . . later his boiling blood dictated passionate beats, then at last, the organ majestically rang with the triumphant rhythm of the Wedding March from *Lohengrin*. The doomed youth was now redeemed: he had played out his whole miserable life."[18] The girl is "awakened" by her husband-to-be and leaves. When the organist looks up, he notices the couple as they embrace at the church's doorsteps. Thoroughly exhausted, he departs and starts coughing. Before he disappears around the corner, in a symbolic gesture of self-destruction he lights a cigarette.

At the beginning of the story Molnár's style is ironic and marked by the frequent use of leitmotifs from nature, but as the pathetic, ill-fated hero begins playing, the tone changes: it becomes exalted, containing questions, repetitions, and exclamations. "Poor, wretched little teacher! Oh, how fiery was his music! He must have compressed all the consumptive fever of many a lonely night into this one march. . . . 'How come?' the fleshy girl pondered, this skinny, shriveled, scrawny scum . . . filling such a huge church . . . where's he got the strength for it?"[19] As the girl departs, there is another shift in the author's tone: now the musical expert Molnár talks, analyzing the young man's technique and the still-reverberating musical pieces, in a dry, professional manner. In the concluding paragraph, however, the language is again highly poetic, rich in images and metaphors which allude to the hero's total abandon and subsequent death-wish. Molnár's heavy use of seemingly incongruous symbols, and the frequent shifts of tone and focus, may confuse the reader at first, but the story is so poignant and poetic that in the end the ambiguities appear to be subtleties that further enhance the fine texture of the tale.

In "The Gnome and the Princess" Molnár adroitly fuses the erotic and the grotesque as he presents yet another anguished young man who is ruthlessly deserted by a woman. The plot is quite simple: In a god-forsaken small mining-town the news arrives one day that a mysterious young lady wishes to visit the coalmine. She turns out to be a little known actress touring the country. A Quasimodo-like, grotesque, myopic journalist, the "Gnome," volunteers to accompany the guest to the "lower depths." Overwhelmed by the actress's charm, the sensitive young man falls in love with her at first sight. In the dark, poorly illuminated tunnels of the mine she freely flirts with the lovelorn youth, but in the daylight dismisses him cruelly.

In this story Molnár's technique is quite ambitious. An almost rough, naturalistic sketch of the filthy, desolate mining town is followed by a fluid, warm, and lengthy characterization of the gnome. The writer meticulously selects several colorful phrases for presenting the unsightly antihero in the most advantageous

light. Each passage describing his physical defects is followed
by another one emphasizing his brilliant mind, noble nature,
sensitivity, and depth. Despite Molnár's understatements—even
euphemisms—concerning his appearance, it is obvious to the
reader that the red-haired gnome is extremely ugly and blends in
well with the forbidding environment. The introduction of the
actress is sketchy, almost superficial. Molnár uses only a few in-
substantial adjectives to describe her, as if to suggest that any
female from the outside world would have the same effect on
the young journalist.

Up to this point the story has a flawless, naturalistic setting,
and serious characterization. Now comes the Molnáresque twist:
the love-scene in the narrow, eerie coal-pit borders on hilarity.
Though the comic elements are underlined here to the limit, the
humor is grotesque and black. When the rather long, romantic,
and erotic episode concludes, the narrator takes over once more.
This time pathos and irony mingle in the tone. As the symbolic
title and frequently employed metaphors suggest, this story was
composed with aesthetic and psychological goals in mind, not
with the object of portraying a certain social milieu or a strange
couple. Undoubtedly, Molnár wants to elicit from his readers
feelings of compassion, sympathy, and concern for the deformed
young man. At the very end he emerges as the symbol of all
men, while the "princess" personifies the evil traits of the Molnáresque "everywoman."

The following two stories are loose, picturesque vignettes
the writer populated with some of his favorite characters.
Molnár rarely slept during the night, and with the brushstroke
of an Impressionistic painter he vividly recreated the night
atmosphere in "The Sons of the Night" and "Winter Morning."
First Molnár lists the advantages of living and working at night
in the manner of a true "addict" (peace, fewer people, better
services at the cafés, etc.), then he draws a series of portraits of
inveterate debauchees and fellow revelers. After exhausting
frolicking (or working), the sons of the night usually tumble
into Turkish baths in the morning to soak and rest their tired
bodies. In these "humid Purgatories" the fatigued, faceless men,
aristocratic gamblers, café residents, hustlers, and street-sweepers
lazily unite, chafing and rubbing each other in otiose cama-

raderie. So intense is their relaxation in the steamy oblivion that they fail to notice a floating body. Someone must have suffered a heart attack. When the corpse is removed, the bathers fall back into their reverie, unperturbed. With artistic abandon, Molnár adorns this cosmopolitan miscellany of night people with vibrant, precisely fitting adjectives. Some of these profligate bathers are presented as transparent, slimy, wrinkled embryos, "members of an all enveloping, intrauteral sect," some as "overgrown, sorrowful, etiolated, yellow flowers." His picturesque description of the languid, half-naked male mob submerging in the frothy water is so lifelike that it affects the reader's sensory nerves. These two tales provide a unique apotheosis of reveling and laziness.

The autobiographical "Goldwatch and Chain" is a very short, playful dialogue featuring some of Molnár's relatives. Following his aunt's funeral, the young Ferenc witnesses the mourners rushing, like vultures, to plunge into the dead woman's "treasures." The tears are still on their cheeks as they throng, shove, and push to grab the pile of trinkets. Their covetousness almost leads to a fistfight over the only really valuable item: a gold watch. Through the rapid, monosyllabic exchange of words, Molnár's relatives become alive, and this truly despicable lot is viewed with astute wit and unconcealed cynicism.

More than half of the short stories in *Music* present women in a variety of roles. In "The Mysterious Csókai" the ingenious heroine invents a phantom lover to foment her husband's jealousy. In "Ribiszke" a cheerful, plump prostitute accompanies her customer on a trip, but instead of providing fun, she acts the lady, imitating the "proper" wife whom he is desperately trying to forget. In "Discretion" an elegant, well-to-do lady tricks a passionate admirer into revealing a minor family secret, then indignantly dismisses him for being a gossip. In all these tales women dominate both the plot and their male partners.

For the second short-story collection, *Three in One*, Molnár borrowed the title from old almanacs which used to contain a calendar, record of past events, and miscellaneous tales. His volume has thirty short stories, impressions and commentaries. Their subject matters do not deviate considerably from the earlier stories: capricious, strong, and selfish females and their often-

humiliated male counterparts trying to surmount their weak-
nesses. In addition, Molnár attacks provincialism and narrow-
mindedness; contrasts honesty with corruption, rich with poor,
pure with evil, reworking some of his newspaper articles on a
loftier plane. The impressions and commentaries are rapid-fire
vignettes of various Budapest types: foxy lawyers, cunning
gamblers, tempestuous actresses caught in humorous or sorrowful
imbroglios. Two stories from this volume are particularly noteworthy.

"The Magician and the Little Servant" is a pathos-filled fable
of a love affair between two outcasts. The plot is variegated but
not overly complex: In one of the Budapest slums lives a slightly
retarded vagrant, Maurer, supporting himself by performing
"magic" and fortune-telling. One day, a young illiterate servant,
Erzsi, comes by and watches him act. Mesmerized by his tricks,
she falls in love with him, gives up her job, and follows the
strange bum everywhere, sharing his despondency and the
mockery he has to endure. Not even brutal physical abuses can
dissuade her. With the abnegation of medieval saints, she humbly
sacrifices her life for a lover who barely tolerates her. Ultimately,
they are chased out of town, and when Maurer is arrested for
burglary she commits suicide.

Molnár's presentation of the principal characters and their
suffering is pervaded by compassion and benign irony: descriptions of the destitution and misery of the slum districts are
considerably more dramatic because there the author's customary naturalism is hauntingly accurate. It has been often said
that a writer succeeds best when he writes about a milieu he
knows intimately. Molnár's familiarity with lumpenproletarian
environments is minimal at best. Yet, his descriptions ring true,
and the dialogues of his low-class protagonists sound natural and
authentic. The writer's fondness for the simple, pure, utterly
devoted servants, who love unconditionally, is apparent. Not
only is the theme, the setting, and the atmosphere of this gemlike
tale reminiscent of *Liliom*, but so are the characters: as the
tragic little Erzsi is a sister of the legendary Juli; Maurer is a
spiritual brother of Liliom.

Molnár's keen perception of the feminine psyche is revealed
in "Princess Olga at the Funeral." A nineteen-year-old beautiful

Russian princess, Olga, goes to Paris to find a cure for her afflic-
tion: she is suffering from unrequited love. Frustrated by the
unabating heartache, she devises odd schemes to ameliorate her
condition and exorcize boredom. One day she decides to attend
the funeral of an unknown neighbor, a young lady who committed suicide because of her husband's unfaithfulness. Dressed
in black, heavily veiled, she joins the procession of mourners,
sobbing loudly at her own misery. The stranger is spotted by
grief-ridden relatives who take her for the mysterious lover who
enticed the husband and caused the tragedy. The mob assaults
Olga, furiously beating her and shoving the almost unconscious
girl into a ditch. A few days after the incident, shaken out of
melancholy, a sad but much wiser princess prepares to return
home.

The plot is somewhat sentimental but the descriptions are
first rate, and so is the structure. The story can be divided into
two parts: the first is a psychological analysis of a complex young
woman; the other, a situation comedy. The tone is serious in
the first, satiric in the second; in each, the writer acts both as
spectator and as critic. The physical setting, although picturesque, is insignificant; the scene of this melodrama is Olga's
soul. In probing the multileveled female psyche, Molnár displays
thorough knowledge of modern psychology, analyzing every
nuance of the heroine's "bleeding heart" with almost scientific
expertise in Freudian terms. The writer proves in this tale that he
can make good use of fashionable trends without becoming a
slave to their formulas.

In the second part the narrator shifts the focus from Olga
to the mourning Frenchmen. The scene where the woebegone,
crying relatives desert the hearse and start punching and pinching the intruder, is particularly humorous. The outraged group
keeps hurling mud as well as expletives at the princess. Then,
after a "job well done" the mourners revert to their tears and
rush to catch up with the glass carriage bearing their "dear dead."

In summation, like Molnár's dramatic works, his short stories
both in *Music* and in *Three in One* are always entertaining.
They often end in anticlimactic jest he is fond of appending to
the more pathetic or serious scenes so that people do not feel
their essential bitterness. In the opinion of a Hungarian-American

scholar, George Halasz, Molnár's tales are "sugarcoated laxatives for the soul, delicious and always effective."[20] The artistic excellence of a few masterpieces minimize the disappointing impact of the somewhat weaker, trivial tales in both collections. In the shadow of his towering dramatic accomplishments, Molnár's narrative ability, too, merits praise: in fact, some of his short stories belong among the classics of the genre.

CHAPTER 4

Molnár the Novelist: From The Hungry City to Autumn Journey

I Introduction

MOLNÁR had no intention of becoming either a playwright or a novelist. While attending law school in Geneva, however, he met Péter Heim, an erudite, enthusiastic Francophile, who talked about Maupassant, Zola, and Flaubert, and who so inspired Molnár that he started to write short stories and prepared outlines for a novella, *Magdolna*.[1] At the same time, he wrote articles covering various political and cultural events in Geneva, and when he returned to Budapest he discovered his true calling.

His instantaneous success as a journalist, the fervent literary activities at the cafés, as well as the example of his mentors at the *Budapesti Napló*—Bródy, Ambrus, and Heltai, all well-known novelists—contributed to Molnár's decision to turn to fiction. During 1898 and 1899, he returned to Western Europe, which he considered "the Mecca of modern novelists." While traveling in Switzerland, Germany, and France, he completed *The Hungry City* and began *The Derelict Boat*. Although *The Hungry City*'s enthusiastic reception was due, to a large extent, to the fact that it had been written abroad, it nevertheless heralded the twenty-one-year-old author as a promising novelist.

Subsequently Molnár wrote twelve novels, half of which were published between 1901 and 1907, and the rest at uneven intervals in the following forty years. At the time of their publication these books were widely popular, yet in literary histories Molnár's name is missing among the Hungarian novelists: he is listed only as the author of the "immortal" juvenile story *The Paul Street Boys*. Some scholars contend that with more

critical conscience and deeper penetration into substance, Molnár could have developed into a novelist *par excellence*; his
early prose revealed a potential for creative eminence "but the
lure of money and success proved stronger than the call of a
true artist, so he eventually sank into prosaic mediocrity."[2]
Ultimately, in this genre, too, Molnár remained faithful to his
artistic credo: he aspired solely to be an entertainer. Treading
on this path, he continued the Hungarian realistic narrative
tradition of the late nineteenth century, but he had no significant
links with any fashionable literary movements of the period.
As an avid reader, he was familiar with and an admirer of the
works of Zola, Maupassant, Dumas, France, Rolland, Keller,
Tolstoy, and Dostoevsky, but their works rather more inspired
than influenced his prose. Molnár's novels indeed reflected the
trends of literature that held sway in Europe at the time; namely,
Naturalism, Neo-Romanticism, Impressionism, and the Freudian
psychoanalytical views. But he utilized the tenets of these new
styles only when and insofar as they suited his purpose.

At the time when Molnár began writing novels, the discussion
of sexual relationship was taboo in Hungarian letters. Previous
writers rendered it only in a diluted form. Molnár severed the
ties with the prudish past and made sex the topical center of
his novels and dramas. Since Freudianism was at its initial
stage, it was not conscious Freudianism but mere intuition that
made Molnár a pioneer in this field. He realized that this universal subject offered countless variations. Thus, almost every
Molnár novel is an appraisal from a different angle of the inces-
santly raging battle of the sexes. The only notable exception is
The Paul Street Boys, in which sensuous love played no role.

II *An Ambitious Start*: The Hungry City

Molnár's first major novel, a *roman à clef*, was published in
1901 and its controversial reception ironically forecast his fate
as an artist. *The Hungry City* had a bombshell effect: it pro-
voked venomous attacks from both the literary critics and the
leaders of the Establishment. At the same time, the book reaped
an unprecedented popular success and made the little-known
Budapest reporter a nationwide celebrity.

Molnár's bold, sincere novel was written in the style of a pamphleteer and presented an impressive catalogue of those human frailties, social ills, and economic inadequacies that used to occupy the columns of young liberal journalists of the time. In the opinion of a leading contemporary critic, Aladár Schöpflin, the novel was "saturated with overzealous, sometimes juvenile enthusiasm, and exaggerations of an idealistic novice-novelist eager to put across a social message. Still, it portended a promising writer."[3]

Paul Orsovai, the novel's hero, is the prototype of the Hungarian white-collar worker: a young, struggling bank clerk without vice or talent whose sole ambition is to make the world forget his low-class Jewish origin and be accepted by Budapest society. When he contracts bronchitis and his doctor orders a change of climate, Paul leaves for an Adriatic resort on borrowed money. At Abbazia he meets Elly Hutchinson, a wealthy American girl traveling in Europe with her father. After a brief, listless courtship, he finds himself married to one of the world's greatest fortunes. When Budapest hears of Orsovai's extraordinary good luck, the whole city is overcome by frenzy and prepares a hero's welcome. "People became hysterical; engulfed in greed, ministers, businessmen, even the clergy, plotted and planned, schemed and conspired toward one end: to get hold of his money. Upon arrival home, they gave Paul the loudest ovation in recent history."[4]

Unseen and unheralded, a poor Italian dock-worker, Ambrosio Posi arrives by the same train, looking for work. Failing to cheer for the celebrity, he is promptly arrested for vagrancy. From here on Posi's penniless, hapless existence runs oddly parallel with the luxuriant, aimless life of the overnight nabob.

No sooner is Paul settled in his new home than he is besieged by sycophants from all walks of life intent on begging, stealing, or bribing him out of the Hutchinson millions. For money he can buy everything: membership into exclusive literary societies and clubs, titles and privileges that place him among the country's elite.

But, as the cliché goes, not even Midas's fortune can buy happiness; shortly Elly realizes that Paul married her only for money. Disgusted by his shallowness and the naked avarice of

the city, she decides to divorce him. Anna, the only woman
Paul ever loved, is also lost: she now lives in marital bliss, and
even his most tempting offers fail to win her from her husband.
Deserted by Elly, longing for Anna, the disconsolate hero commits suicide a day before he is to be elected representative in
the Parliament. His body is taken to the city morgue and there,
once more, fate links him with another lonely mortal, Posi, whose
starved body is also brought in that same night. The two men,
who lived a world apart, seemed to share their unhappiness,
caused by too much money or the lack of it.

The Hungry City, though not published in English, is perhaps one of Molnár's most sincere, noncynical, unpretentious
works. It is also his most sustained effort at social satire; but
the writer does not fully exploit the rich possibilities latent in
his theme, nor does he succeed in creating a "burlesque of the
Bildungsroman" as was his plan. Molnár failed primarily in the
portrayal of the protagonist, Julien Sorel's Hungarian alter-ego.
Instead of depicting the complete downfall and ruin of this
immoral social climber, and pursuing his career to the bitter
end by showing how the money-craving city deserts its penniless son, Molnár resolved the conflict by a convenient suicide.
The characterization of the two Americans is also superficial
and unrealistic: they do not seem to have language problems in
Hungary and Elly's quick adjustment to a strange culture seems
improbable at best.

Instead, though the book expands on a cavalcade of sharply
drawn minor characters, caricatures of corrupt statesmen, cunning politicians, seamy businessmen, demoralized judges, bribed
editors, and immoral bishops. Molnár's stylistic idiosyncrasies
are geared to convey more energy than reflection. The large array
of people who tumble through Orsovai's life are more remarkable than remarked upon and make the book cluttered with
irrelevant details. Events and people swirl like unanchored
pinwheels, often to dazzling effect, but most portraits remain
rough-and-ready sketches only. Perhaps the character of Ambrosio Posi is an exception. The destitute Italian is presented with
straightforward realism; both his personality and predicament
are credible and genuinely moving.

Even the description of Budapest, Molnár's native sphere, is hurried and somewhat uneven. What made the novel an instant bestseller was the satiric and often hilarious characterization, the arrogantly outspoken critical tone and the fluent style, but this also reduced it to a typical period piece because "only contemporary readers could revel in trying to identify who the disguised fictional figures were in real life."[5] Incidentally, not even the most meticulous scholars can recognize the characters today. Thus, the novel's salutory qualities lie rather in its potential artistry than in the full realization of its artistic potentialities.

III *Lovelorn Ladies, the Losers*

In view of Molnár's fascination with women it was not surprising that most of his novels centered around female protagonists modeled after his lovers. The author frequently transposed his private conflicts into his art, but his novels appeared even more conspicuously autobiographical than his plays. In fact, Molnár used this genre as self-cure for his occasional depression. Each time he suffered a deep wound—genuine or imagined—in the forever-raging combats with the "weaker sex," he turned to prose. During his career Molnár seemingly wrote novels either to find solace and purge himself through reliving some dramatic events in his life, as in *Andor* or *Autumn Journey*; or to repent publicly for the pains he had inflicted by immortalizing the injured partners into romantic heroines, as in *The Derelict Boat*, *The Green Hussar*, and others. These fictitious ladies, unlike their devious, domineering counterparts in the short stories and dialogues, were presented as victims of love and circumstances beyond their control. Thus, Molnár's early narrative works were devoid of humor and generally considered tragic. Four such novels are representative: *Egy gazdátlan csónak története* (The Derelict Boat) (1901), *Eva* (1903) *Egy pesti lány története* (Story of a Budapest Girl) (1905), and *Rabok* (Prisoners) (1907).

The Derelict Boat, published less than a year after *The Hungry City*, was unanimously well received. This short, poetic novel, a psychological study of an adolescent girl's first love, proved Molnár an accomplished prose artist. Eighteen years later, when he elaborated it into a play, *Heavenly and Earthly Love*, the book became popular in Hungary again and later attracted foreign publishers as well.[6]

The simple plot focuses on fifteen-year-old Pirkó Wald, a precocious, highly sensitive, and slightly neurotic girl. She spends summer vacation with a friend on the *Margitsziget*, in mid-Danube between Buda and Pest. There she meets Andy Tarkovics, a thirty-two-year-old cynical, Bohemian journalist. The young girl, impressed by Andy's age, looks, and sophistication, falls desperately in love with him, savoring the soul-searching and suffering of hidden and unrequited love. He is bemused by the girl's attention and "adult philosophizing"; their conversations grow in length and intensity and so does her adulation. However, when Pirkó feels she is about to win his heart, her flamboyant, sensuous mother returns unexpectedly from Paris. It soon becomes apparent that Andy's attention to Pirkó was only a pretext: his real object was to get closer, through the daughter, to Mrs. Wald, the only woman the journalist ever loved. The utterly devastated girl sneaks out one stormy night, dressed in a long white gown, unties a rowboat, and lets herself be swept off by the raging waves. At dawn, perplexed oarsmen of a nearby barge spot the derelict boat and discover the tragedy.

Despite its brevity, *The Derelict Boat* has complexity that lends itself to multileveled interpretation. The novel, it has been said, was inspired by actual experience. Whether or not this assertion is true, one thing is certain: Tarkovics's character contains many traits of Molnár. He, too, was a carefree journalist defying authorities, scoffing at the gods and old values. The hero, like his creator, was an unconventional cynic and a Heine enthusiast, perpetually seeking pleasure. The womanizer social lion Molnár was also rumored to have prompted the suicide of a lovelorn lady.[7] And the book's bucolic setting was his favorite haven; he sought refuge on the island periodically every year.

The novel's significance lies not in the autobiographical curiosities but in its poetic style. Molnár makes use of familiar literary allusions to create a melancholy mood throughout. Pirkó's tragic purity reminds us of Hauptmann's Hannele; her drowning in a resplendent white dress brings to mind Ophelia's death;

she rocks herself onto the other shore of the River Styx (the Danube), summoned by luring sounds coming from the billows, as was Wagner's Senta. Pirkó's wailing: "I do want to suffer, it's so good for me!" could have been uttered by Goethe's Ottilie or any other romantic heroine. These devices and the theme lend the story a romantic aura even though characterization and the descriptive parts are realistic, showing touches of Naturalism.

The presentation of Pirkó's personality and her tragic plight is resonant with Freudian echoes: a fatherless girl's infatuation with a much older man, hatred and jealousy for the mother, and an almost clinical analysis of a neurotic teen-ager's mounting anxieties. The psychological profile of the adolescent in transition is drawn with systematic, nearly scientific precision. The reader can follow the process as the tormented, confused soul is at first torn between, then falls victim to, the most profound opposites. Like her peers, Pirkó knows no moderation. But her emotions are not simply extreme, they are pathological: her passion borders on the manic and her sadness edges close to depression. If we read the novel as a confrontation between filial attachment and sensuous love, we may find that the book's translator, Emil Lengyel, underscores the heroine's motivation when he observes; "The soul of this young girl vibrates more readily to every little affection because she is a delicate instrument, created to respond to every melody of love's symphony."[8]

The structure is clear and firm: the first part shows how love has ripened into an all consuming passion in her soul. The second part is an intense, dramatic narration which explains and leads to Pirkó's tragic fall. Demonstrating Molnár's psychological insight, this essentially romantic story can be regarded as a small masterpiece.

While *The Derelict Boat* met favorable reception, Molnár's next novel, *Eva*, was less successful and evoked minimal response. Its plot was allegedly based on a true story the author claimed to have heard during one of his rare trips in the highlands.

The setting is a tiny, remote, grim, Slovakian mining town where the sudden appearance of a city-bred, voluptuous divorcée causes an emotional uproar unparalleled by the worst explosion the silver mine has ever known. Eva's presence drastically changes everyone's life. Each member of the mine's small directorial staff falls in love with the attractive visitor; in the rivalry for her favors, friends become enemies and dull bureaucrats emerge as passionate political activists. Eva gets burned, too. But when the succession of events portends actual violence and more than one death occurs, she departs, leaving behind scores of broken hearts and the germ of a revolt.

We may regard *Eva* a "laboratory" experiment in which the ingredients, while taken from life, represent materials particularly suitable for analytical purposes. The story is a dramatic evidence of the thesis that love is paramount both when life is primitive and when it is complicated. The novel's best feature is Molnár's portrayal of the heavy, "humid" atmosphere in a sex-hungry world saturated with frustration and desire. Eva's characterization reveals both the fascination and revulsion the author feels for such all-powerful females: she comes across as a primordial Eve, the archetypal temptress. The style is informal and somewhat rambling but the tense mood is artistically sustained.

The Story of a Budapest Woman is the weakest novel of this group. It describes the colorful career of a "modern" girl, Elza Brandt, a frivolous, wealthy debutante, who regards love as a mere pastime until she meets her "Rhett Butler," Nick Gál, a starving bank clerk. Since he is too poor to provide for her, she marries a rich old lawyer. Driven by her passion, she commits adultery and soon ends up a lurking figure of the street-corners, but in the end the two outcasts of Budapest society resume their affair.

Molnár himself dismissed this banal, hastily put together work as a "careless experiment," admitting that it was written for money only. After one small edition in Hungary, a revised version under a different title was published in Germany.[9]

Prisoners, a combination of love story and social criticism, went almost unnoticed in Hungary, but its English translation several years later attracted considerable attention: it had a large edition and was made into a motion picture.[10] The novel's subject matter was taken from the daily logs Molnár had kept as a court reporter.

The elegant Nicholas Chathy is happily engaged to Lenke Rimmel, daughter of the Chief Warden at the Municipal Prison. In the course of his first important case, however, Chathy becomes emotionally involved with his pretty client, Riza Nagy, a thief, who has been a waitress at the lawyer's frequented café. During counseling, she confesses her love for him; apparently she resorted to crime only to attract his attention. Riza is a wild, hysterical creature willing to sacrifice physical freedom for the liberation of her soul. She is determined to go to prison as long as he recognizes her affection. Chathy defends her bravely and his speech turns into an open declaration of love. The judge is moved and reduces the sentence to seven months imprisonment. When the girl is escorted to the very prison where Lenke resides behind starched curtains and a wall of innocence, Chathy reasons that true freedom prevails only in Riza's cell, while outside live the real convicts, prisoners of prejudice and false morality. He breaks up with the lovesick Lenke and awaits the reunion with his "jailbird."

The original purpose of *Prisoners* was to unveil the brazen corruption and double standards reigning within the Hungarian penal system. Instead, Molnár produced a well-constructed but naive tale and a "reorganization" of platitudes concerning prisons and prisoners. The novel's basic premise is false, its conflict sounds tendentious, and the main characters come across as shallow stereotypes. The style is fluent and not altogether inartistic, but the symbolical overtone suggested by the title enhances neither the plot nor the theme. As usual, Molnár is deft in the dialogues; the most interesting parts are the presentation of the clientele and the rendition of the atmosphere in the Bohemian sidewalk café where the heroine used to work. Essentially the novel is no more than an additional tribute to passionate love a la Molnár.

IV *The Zenith*: The Paul Street Boys

Published in 1907, Molnár's most celebrated work of prose, *The Paul Street Boys*, has since made many eyes grow misty all over the world. This poignant story of two juvenile street gangs became a classic and has remained one of Hungary's most popular books. It was translated into fourteen languages (receiving two different English versions),[11] adapted for stage, and made into movies in various countries.[12]

The novel was conceived in a typical Molnáresque fashion. In 1906, a few weeks before his wedding, the bridegroom realized that he was short of money. What was the quickest way to make it? By writing a novel in a hurry. So he did. Since there was no time to work out a complicated plot, he assembled a few sketches from his volume *Children* and expanded the longest one, "The Putty Club." Night after night, sitting in the "serene" atmosphere of the "New York Café," Molnár recalled his own childhood spent on the neighboring playground on Paul Street. The novel appeared serialized in a teen-age magazine,[13] and its reception was reminiscent of the wild anticipation with which Americans greeted each installment of Dickens's *Little Dorrit* around 1857.

The book is about a group of youngsters and their "gang"—a microcosm of society. Their country is the playground on Paul Street where they reconstruct the world of adults. In reality, this vacant lot, called "the *grund*," is owned by a lumber company, but the boys feel they possess in it a miraculous piece of land which, according to their mood and the requirement of the game, is continually changing in their imagination from mountains to prairies, from ocean beach to blood-drenched battlefields. "To the child of Budapest [the *grund*] is his open country, his grassland, his plains. To him it spells freedom and boundlessness, this plot of ground that is hedged about by a rickety fence on one side, and by rearing walls stabbing skyward on the others."[14] The Paul Street gang is headed by Bóka, "the fair and humane general," and the members are colonels, captains, and lieutenants. Besides the guard's dog, the only other private is Ernő Nemecsek, the book's diminutive hero. The wretched youth is forever taunted and never gains his ends because "to most people [he] was thin air; like the figure one in arithmetic, he neither multiplied nor divided things. No one paid attention to him. He was an insignificant, lean and weak-kneed youngster. It was probably this very inferiority which made him an ideal victim."[15] There are always notations against him in the gang's Black Book, but nothing serious even as things go in this strict "military organization." The little loser, never discouraged, keeps striving to earn an officer's cap.

One day he detects Feri Áts, the feared leader of the Red Shirts, the rival gang, stealing their flag. This is an open declaration of war. As both groups begin preparation for the attack, Geréb, Bóka's antagonist among the Paul Street Boys, decides to defect and join the other gang. Nemecsek discovers the foul play and follows the traitor to the enemy's headquarters. There, hiding on a tree, he overhears Geréb betraying their tactics, and the subsequent strategy meeting of the Red Shirts. In a dramatic moment, mustering extreme courage, he reveals himself to the whole gang, each member of which is older, stronger, and tougher than himself. This heroic deed earns him respect among the big boys, but still the spy has to be punished. The frail boy bravely endures three "forced plunges" in the icy water of a nearby pond and catches pneumonia.

On the day of the battle, the gravely ill little private escapes from bed, and the sudden appearance of a figure wrapped in blankets in the fight's crucial moment causes such confusion that the almost-beaten Paul Street Boys win. The hero collapses. Bóka and Áts bring him home and together they keep vigil at his deathbed. Nemecsek dies happily after having been promoted to the rank of captain, never knowing that his "country," the *grund*, is forever gone: construction is about to begin; a new apartment building will be erected on the empty lot.

Nemecsek symbolizes heroic sacrifice; the fragile, downtrodden little fellow endows with true community spirit the world of teen-agers. Even in his last moments the duty to his friends, to his *grund*, to his club, to this society are foremost on his delirious mind. Before his death, the little private metamorphoses into a true hero and leaves a legacy for all young boys to strive for.

The description of his dying moments demonstrates Molnár's remarkable creative ability, sensitivity, and artistic power. Nemecsek's father is a poor tailor. As the boy lies mortally ill, a customer comes to try on a suit. From the next room, the youth's final agonizing hallucination, as he lives over again the gigantic battle fought on the *grund*, comes through to the grief-ridden father while he is painstakingly trying to please a fussy

customer. This kind of counterpoint conveys a sense of grotesque, pathetic, and ironic interplay of ordinary life; in such
techniques the writer is at his best. When the child dies, the
tailor sinks beside the bed, weeping, "But even now," Molnár
writes, "he was not unmindful of Mr. Csetneky's handsome
brown jacket; he slipped it off his knee, so as to prevent it
from being stained by tears."[16]

The book is populated with realistically portrayed children
playing adults; they are deadly serious, and so is Molnár in recounting their genuine nobility, innocence, idealism, love of
freedom, camaraderie, loyalty, and also their inherent cruelty.
The gang life is an allegory: the troubled childhood incapsu-
lates the problem-ridden age. The *grund* is a metaphor for their
insatiable yearning for freedom; it is the battlefield of youth,
mischief, ambitions, of small pleasure and self-willed forces.

The passages depicting the gang war are interwoven with
images of Romanticism of the Indian Wars (fortress, lantern,
dungeon, tomahawk), echoing both the strong Cooper craze
in Hungary at that time, and Molnár's admiration for Mark
Twain. Critics often compare this work with *Tom Sawyer* and
Huckleberry Finn, as well as with Edmondo de Amicis' *Cuore*
because of the similar effect they had upon the public.[17]

Throughout the novel, Molnár maintains balance and credibility: the precise, realistic descriptions counterbalance the
sentimentality of the theme. He also measures out Romanticism
and Naturalism carefully, keeping episodes, dialogues, and
descriptions in proper balance. The writer's insight of young
people's psyche is communicated to the reader in a succinct,
poetic style.

V   *The Anticlimax*: Andor

During the last two years of World War I, overcome by
anguish and disillusionment, Molnár wrote his longest (621
pages) and darkest novel, *Andor*, allegedly based on the life of
Sándor Mester, editor of the *Pesti Napló*. After a mixed reception, the book was soon forgotten and no English translation
has been made. Recently, however, Marxist critics reevaluated
its ideological significance and revived the public's interest.

Of more importance is the novel's difference from other works. It is Molnár's most detailed portrayal of a male protagonist's futile attempt to free himself from his congenital enervation and gain control over his future.

The protagonist's life parallels in many respects the author's own life, and Molnár seems to have projected his character into the novel for therapeutic reasons. Unfortunately, he failed to sustain the reader's interest in the hero's inane, idle existence.

This expansive novel is devoid of true action. The twenty-one-year-old Andor only endures languidly the minor events befalling him and seldom resorts to active participation. Molnár's exposition of the weary hero simultaneously sets the mood and delineates the background. The story takes place in Budapest, spanning five years in the 1910s, featuring Andor Aradi, a bright, handsome young man in an enervated pursuit of a goal in his life. At the beginning we learn that Andor's mother died early and his wealthy father is mortally ill; alienated both from family and society, he tries to embark upon a career. He first becomes a lawyer, then a journalist, and even a short-term politician. But with him everything is temporary and aimless. He quits every job without having any idea of what to do next. Molnár treats his hero with unmitigated irony: "Andor considered his stagnant life-style only transitory; each Monday everything was supposed to change but nothing did; he couldn't tell why but he felt too fatigued to ponder about it; he postponed decision-making till tomorrow; next morning however, restlessness came over him—a dangerous state of mind—so he brushed aside all thoughts and stretched out sensuously in his worn, cradle-like bed."[18] To kill time, he plunges into uninhibited carousing. He gambles and drinks to excess, subsisting on two or three hours of sleep. For no apparent reason, he jilts his ordinary and loyal fiancée, Ella, and accepts the altruistic worship of a bellydancer. While their haphazard affair lasts, he carries on a suffocating, platonic relationship with a frustrated rich girl. Soon Andor leaves them both and again becomes infatuated with Ella, now engaged to his friend. Following her wedding and his father's death, Andor attempts suicide. After recovery, the lonely, isolated hero chases the newlyweds, reveling in his masochism while watching their happiness. Next he aimlessly saunters from place to place, locates an old family servant, Juli, and moves in with her family. When Juli's teen-age daughter falls in love with the elegant, gentle guest, her jealous boyfriend stabs the intruder. Andor's recuperation in a plush sanatorium marks the time of final reckoning: not having any purpose in life, the burned-out man shoots himself at the age of twenty-six.

Andor's ennui is a form of moral insanity, a manifestation of an existential urban neurosis. Incapable of genuine affection, he unintentionally destroys everyone who comes into contact with him. Without any reason, he cynically betrays friends, double-crosses supporters, and abandons lovers. His attempts to change his life-style are as futile as they are ardent. Underneath the tranquil facade, perpetual inner wars rage, but his sentimental self-analyses lead nowhere: like an antihero in an absurd play, Andor is nervously waiting for nothing in particular. Yet, he maintains his sharp critical ability. Posing as Hamlet, he sees the problems and knows what should be done, but he is incapable of action. The reader wonders: Is he a victim of overwhelming outside pressures or simply a decadent weakling, a stereotype of his class or an individual degenerate? Is *Andor* indeed meant to be Molnár's comprehensive social criticism of the disintegrating bourgeoisie or a mere experimentation with fictional psychoanalysis of a man?

Critics offer vastly different interpretations. Contemporary literary scholars compare the novel to Goncharov's *Oblomov* and Flaubert's *Sentimental Education*. Géza Hegedüs views *Andor* as "a bona fide critical-realistic epic masterpiece featuring an authentic type of the declining bourgeoisie."[19] Irén Vécsei agrees, deeming the book to be a naturalistic social satire in which Molnár repudiates tepid middle-class impotency and mourns, at the same time, the lost illusions with sad resignation.[20] George Lukács, the outstanding Marxist aesthete, however, disparages *Andor* as "a boring, sentimental glorification of an average Budapest bourgeois's life and his inherited purposelessness." In his opinion, the hero has no philosophy: his nihilism is only a pose disguising his degeneration.[21] A compromise is possible, concurring with both camps. Criticisms, though disparate in thematic interpretation, correspond in praising the novel's consummate structure and Molnár's unique skill in utilizing many Freudian concepts effectively. The pervading stifling atmosphere, as well as the melancholy mood, is sustained throughout. The novel's stylistic and tonal unity are provided by an artistic synthesis: a felicitous blend of cynicism and sentimentality; lithe, fluid dialogues and complex internal monologues; short, staccato phrases and torrentially flowing compound sentences; simple, colloquial talks and eloquent, pseudo-scientific speeches. The reader may feel irritated and occasionally be bored by Andor's *Weltschmerz* and his tedious imitation of the "Oblomovian" Russian otiosity, but the Hungarian ambiance, the incorporated autobiographical confessions, and the painstaking character analysis make the novel intriguing and document Molnár's narrative versatility.

VI *Novels of Nostalgia*

Fifteen years elapsed before Molnár wrote another novel. During the intervening period his mood grew increasingly gloomier. Fame and fortune notwithstanding, the onetime debonair socialite turned into a morose introvert. Advancing in age, bereft of his native city, Molnár registered the social changes even more concernedly than before. He sensed the gradual collapse of his old world and the looming of a new cataclysm. Engulfed in nostalgia for his youth, his beloved Budapest, and all the glory of yore, Molnár turned to the narrative genre and found it again the most auspicious vehicle for alleviating his depression and providing temporary solace. He wrote *A zenélő angyal* (Angel making Music, 1933), *A zöld huszár* (The Green Hussar, 1937), and *Őszi utazás* (Autumn Journey, 1939) in memory of the resplendent past. In these novels, his customary irony and humor appeared less often than anguish and pathos. The tone was subdued; the mood, overly melancholy; and most characters were tragic or rejected.

Angel making Music was the most successful of the three. The peregrinating author moved the locale of his new book to a frequented favorite stopover on his sojourns: the romantic city of Venice, an especially appropriate setting for a sad love story.

Indeed, the overly luxuriant environment and its hothouse atmosphere served as convenient artistic means by which Molnár set the mood and tone. Although combining elements of travelogue and detective story, the novel essentially manifested the author's unabating interest in youth and the feminine psyche. The book was an instant success in Hungary and Italy; its English version also received favorable reviews.

Ultimately this is a one-woman novel. The writer focuses on his heroine's internal conflicts, using other characters and the milieu as props in a psychological drama. A prosperous Hungarian banker's daughter, Irma Lietzen, is vacationing in Venice with her parents. The highly emotional young girl, affected by the romantic surroundings, falls in love with the first man she meets, who happens to be her father's local secretary. Aurél, an expatriate, is bright, earnest, and subserviently polite. The novel's first part is a poetic exploration of how Irma's affection—though utterly devoid of carnality—develops into an all-consuming rapture. The pivotal episodes take place in the second part when the young clerk fails to return her devotion. He prefers the wholesomely sensuous, mature Judith, Mrs. Lietzen's nurse. The two "servants of the rich" soon become lovers. Unrequited love and jealousy all but unhinge Irma's mind and she behaves like a maenad overcharged with schemes of vengeance. She smuggles her mother's diamond brooch into Judith's suitcase to incriminate the unsuspecting girl who is getting ready to escape with Aurél. The last part of the book recounts the proceeds of a nerve-wracking investigation and Irma's agonizing soul-searching. She is beset by twinging guilt, but is too proud to confess. In the end, truth triumphs: the exalted, selfish girl remains alone, and her slandered rival is exonerated and marries Aurél. As the family is leaving Venice, Irma asks to stop at Church Frari. Kneeling before Bellini's *Madonna*, she stares at Judith's favorite painting. When she spots the chubby cherubs with the flute near the Madonna, Irma breaks down and within a few minutes undergoes a complete change. This is the prolonged climax of the tale.

Underneath the multilayered insouciance and suppressed physical desires, she begins to feel a sudden upsurge of sexuality. She realizes that the angel making music is the symbol of women's primordial wish to bear a child. "Her face lit up . . . there . . . there was the fat little music-making angel-child blowing on his flute. A sweet warmth surged through her."[22] Irma discovers Judith's secret, the painting's magic, and her purpose in life.

Molnár's characterization is naturalistic; nothing is withheld: the heroine in close-up stands naked with her physical and metaphysical blisters ruthlessly exposed. Molnár's achievement is that he made this rather superficial character oddly vulnerable, even touching, despite her abominable machinations. The others remain only entertaining cameos: the weak, doting father; the snobbish, hypochondriac, parvenu mother; and the scrupulously honest, warm, feminine Judith. Aurél comes across as a featureless, average youth.

Molnár is eloquent in depicting the setting, the glory of Venice. With realism and rarely displayed artistry, using rich similes and metaphors, he revives the semi-Oriental splendor, the exuberance of Renaissance and Baroque art and architecture, and the golden blue magnificence of "the city of pedestrians." "San Giorgio Maggiore burned red in the sun. As if, from centuries of sunshine, the walls and the green cornices of the brick tower had acquired the burnt, brownish red skin-color of the old fishermen and gondoliers. . . . The Laguna—that distant, sprawling, waveless, false sea—was blue now. The sky still more blue, almost steel blue in the heat. These Latin blues are not afraid of the German word *Kitsch*, they dare to be just as blue as they fancy."[23]

The descriptive parts reflect the artist, who had lived in the city for some time and knew it intimately. The language blends with the setting; it is translucent and sparkling like Venetian glass beads; gently coiling like the canals; facile, lacy, like the Gothic steeples; and miraculously sustained like the buildings on the lagunas.

Concurrent with his adoration of Venice, Molnár's nostalgia for his homeland rises from the pages. During conversations, people keep reminiscing, recalling memories of Budapest and making comparisons: the canals with the Danube, Italian luxury liners with Hungarian steamships, the gondoliers' serenading with Gypsy music, the spicing of Veal Parmesan with *Wiener*

Schnitzel. All through the book the reader can unmistakably sense the author's yearning for his country.

The style is also in harmony with the novel's rich, velvety texture. Irma's outbursts and internal monologues are complex and vibrant with neurotic images. In the direct characterization, however, the language is calm and transparent. Unfortunately, there is a complete change in atmosphere and a break in style in the last part when the police begin investigating the alleged theft. The shift is awkward because Molnár as a sleuth sounds dissonant and a bit sensational. It appears to be a rather cheap and easy form of denouement of a truly artistic and entertaining case history of a young girl's love, or the collision between Platonic love and sensuous passion.

Despite the artistic superiority of *Angel making Music*, Molnár preferred his next novel, *The Green Hussar.* Never published in English, the book is perhaps his saddest autobiographical work of this period. When novelists seek to create characters who will represent their own hidden emotions, they start by delineating something different. It is by wearing a mask that one obtains freedom of self-expression. In Molnár's words: "The works of a real writer contain a great many hidden, adroitly distorted, more or less camouflaged, yet often—because the author feels safe behind the mask—frighteningly honest fragments of autobiography. The better disguised these confessions are, the more honest they will be."[24] *The Green Hussar,* despite the relatively thin disguise, is painfully honest and most revealing. By writing this novel, the almost sixty-year-old writer sought comfort in self-disclosure. The result was a concise (144 pages), tragic love story, a slightly changed version of the events and circumstances surrounding his own attempted suicide in 1910. It must have been a truly memorable event since he had already incorporated part of the story into *Andor* and later into a one-act play, *Marshall.*

The novel is a first-person narrative delivered by an aging journalist recalling the memory of his only true love in retrospect, thirty years later. At twenty-three, during an assignment to cover a story in a small town, he is introduced to a loose waitress, Annie, the local queen of prostitutes. They fall in love overnight. Sensing danger, the still virgin journalist flees back to

Budapest into the arms of his prim and proper fiancée. But the fiery, demonic Annie, completely mesmerized by his elegant reserve, follows him to the capital. Yearning for him, she nevertheless resumes her profession and later moves in with a crippled, possessive photographer. In trying to win Annie's favors, the unfortunate man caters to all her whims and becomes bankrupt in that hopeless endeavor. Meanwhile, she gets a part as an extra in a cabaret, appearing as a hussar clad in a green uniform. The restless journalist is attracted and repelled by emotional rapture: he longs for her but knows their meeting would end in calamity. Feverish with passion, he furtively watches the show, then goes to a party where Annie happens to be a surprise entertainer. The evening almost ends in a scandal when, in a frenzy, she dashes over to him and declares her love, begging the journalist "to raise her from this mud." Petrified by such intensity of emotions, he rebuffs her and runs away, burying his anguish in alcohol and sedatives. A week later, Annie kills herself, leaving behind a farewell note for her "cruel virgin friend," the only man she ever loved. Haunted by remorse, the narrator lives in a blind delirium for a while, then he too, takes an overdose of sleeping pills. "There were still nine packs of veronal-powders in the box. 'I'm yours darling, I'm thinking of you, why aren't you here? I'm coming!' I poured the powders into my tea. . . . That night I learnt what death meant. The fact that they brought me back to life later does not alter the case."[25]

Autumn Journey has a unique place in Molnár's work: it was the last book brought out by his old Budapest publisher, Athenaeum, and it went completely unnoticed in his hometown. Understandably, in 1939 Hungarians were more concerned with the real machinations of Hitler than with a fictitious tale of political and industrial espionage—subject matter also uncharacteristic of the author. Moreover, for the first time in Molnár's career, the American publication of his book was refused on political grounds: Molnár's open admiration for Mussolini's Italy.[26] The rejection was no great loss since the novel offered little that was new.

The plot centers around Margit Nagy, a good-looking, high-strung gentry girl who travels to Venice in search of adventure.

There she meets a middle-aged American banker, Gilbert Carr, who is on a secret mission. They fall in love and Margit accompanies him to Monte Carlo as a secretary. Without having any idea of the nature of her job, she is confronted with her first assignment. She must entertain and pump vital information from a young German industrialist, Walter, the head of a giant war-production concern. The plan fails when Carr, in a fit of jealousy, attacks Walter. To escape investigation, they return to Italy, "the only safe and civilized place left in Europe." Carr is shortly summoned back to London via Nice by his mysterious boss, Kathlyn. She turns out to be his common-law wife, mother of his children, and also head of a large-scale spy-ring. The heartbroken Margit gradually learns the truth. Her lover, an international crook, is arrested at the border, having been denounced by Kathlyn—a safe way to separate the lovers. Abandoned, Margit realizes that the autumn journey meant more than an adventure: it shattered her illusions and changed her life.

On the surface, the novel shows striking resemblances to *Angel making Music*, but artistically it is far inferior. The plot is secondary to the characters and tertiary to the style. The writer spins the colorful thread of his tale effortlessly, but it lacks cohesiveness. The book's original title, *Danubian Seagull*, had suggested Margit's initial purity and her attachment to the Danube that flows near her hometown. The new title, while suited to the story, also ironically symbolizes Molnár's own fate: this was to be the "autumnal" author's very last book written in Europe, during his last journey, in his much-admired Venice. Downcast by the war, Molnár sailed to America soon after the completion of *Autumn Journey*.

Molnár's novels are characterized by stylistic brilliance, cleverly calculated plots, meticulous structure, realistically portrayed characters, and authentic settings. His tone is urban and self-assertive, revealing both his journalistic training in the consistently economic use of words, and his playwriting talent in his fluid dramatic dialogues. In the often autobiographical, character-oriented novels, there are no villains, only erring human beings. A genuinely entertaining but by no means universal novelist, Molnár may be evaluated at his best on the basis of *The Paul Street Boys*, a belletristic masterpiece.

CHAPTER 5

Molnár the Playwright: From The Devil to Delilah

I Native Heritage and Foreign Influence

MOLNÁR's most significant contribution to literature was undoubtedly in the field of drama. He was "the Prince of the Theater," the first Hungarian dramatist to become internationally famous, achieving both critical and financial success at home and abroad. During his artistic career, Molnár wrote forty-two plays, most of them performed all over the world, including Broadway. Twenty-six motion pictures and three musical comedies produced in the United States alone were based on his dramatic works. Despite the handicap of a remote language and a scarcely known culture, he broke out of his native land's literary isolation. By entertaining audiences of many countries, calling their attention to Hungary, and creating a demand for export dramas, his plays made Budapest known as one of the theater centers of the world.

At the turn of the century, when Molnár began writing plays, the old-fashioned patriotic and Romantic conventions still prevailed on the Hungarian stage. In fact, drama was the only genre in the nineteenth century that remained largely unaffected by the new European literary trends. There was hardly any experimental theater in Hungary. On the stage, the spiritual revival was less esoteric than in other branches of literature; it was, in some way, a "middle-brow" revolution, and even as such it was not particularly successful until Molnár became its undisputed leader as the spokesman of the rising bourgeoisie.

Molnár's "stage family-tree" meanders back to Károly Kisfaludy, 100 years his senior, the forefather of Hungarian boulevard authors.[1] Like Molnár, he wrote in cafés and produced

scores of deft, whimsical, light comedies which, at the beginning of the nineteenth century in Hungary, had been considered
rather daring, pioneer pieces. Ede Szigligeti and Gergely Csíky
continued this tradition by writing similar fluid farces, but in
addition they modernized the theater further by introducing
folk dramas (*népszinmű*), thesis plays, and satirical social comedies. Their endeavors paved the way for the Hungarian bourgeois drama which culminated in Molnár's work.[2] These innovative dramatists—who aspired primarily to entertain the public
—must be judged as Molnár's predecessors and precursors of the
Hungarian theater and not as first-rate writers of theatrical literature. During the nineteenth century, only three playwrights
of classic proportion emerged in Hungary: József Katona, Mihály
Vörösmarty, and Imre Madách. Their significance, however,
was by and large limited to national and not to world literature.[3]

Among the contemporaries, Bródy influenced Molnár most
profoundly. At the early stage of his development, Bródy provided encouragement and guided the novice playwright toward
the use of a consistently poetic style in drama. Molnár also
acquired his mentor's Naturalistic method of observing urban
life and his compassion for fine technique and impeccable
craftsmanship.[4]

Despite Molnár's roots in the native dramatic tradition, he
was indeed a modern artist, a trend-setter who soon discarded
inherited patterns, transcended qualities of his Hungarian
models, and violated practically all the conventions of his
country's stage. He expanded Hungary's theatrical horizon by
assimilating new techniques and fashionable dramatic expressions of prominent European playwrights. Yet, his own inventions made the influence more genuine.

At the onset of his dramatic career, French theater left
the longest-lasting impact on Molnár. An ardent Francophile,
he knew and admired the works of Scribe, Sardou, and Dumas
as well as the whole school of boulevard authors: Capus, Bernard, Bataille, Bernstein, Flers, and Caillavet, who dominated
the French stage in the second half of the last century. In Paris
and Geneva he saw their plays and later translated and adapted
dozens of them into Hungarian. From the French he derived

the legacy of verbal wit, polished dialogues, and the bent for unexpected twists.

Of the English stage Molnár knew relatively little; he read the plays only in translation. Still, certain influences were immediately apparent, but the differences were basically greater. Aside from the striking personal resemblance between him and Oscar Wilde—both being handsome, elegant cynics, suave conversationalists, and masters of quirks and paradoxes—Molnár's art revealed conspicuous kinship with the British teaser's frivolous and sarcastic comedies of manners. Between 1905–1910, Wilde's influence was especially strong. Later Molnár preferred George Bernard Shaw, from whom he learned the technique of lengthy stage directions and the proper timing of stage ripostes.

Maeterlinck's Symbolism and mysterious Romanticism, as well as Hauptmann's blend of Realism and Romantic fantasy, can also be traced in Molnár's dramas. Thematically, however, the Austrian Schnitzler's erotic, decadent plays left the deepest impression on him. Molnár adopted the Schnitzlerian motto, "Words lie," as well as his play-acting games. Demonstrating the relativity of truth and the barely discernible difference between illusion and reality became Molnár's major dramatic signature whereby he had preceded and to a certain extent perhaps, even inspired Pirandello.

By fusing Hungarian stage tradition and Western influences into a cosmopolitan amalgam, Molnár appeared a natural-born playwright whose *Zeitgeist*, mesmerizing dramatic instinct, dazzling technique, and vivid style were uniquely his own. In this chapter all his major plays, written between 1902–1937, will be analyzed in chronological order. The length and depth of discussions vary according to the significance of each work. Unless otherwise noted, up to 1929 the citations are taken from *All the Plays of Molnár.*[5]

II *The First Steps*: The Lawyer *and* Józsi

Early in 1902, Molnár was commissioned to write a play for Hungary's most prestigious stage, the Nemzeti Szinház (National Theater). The offer came from its director, László Beőthy, an old friend and former fellow journalist who used to read

Molnár's works regularly. The young reporter's sparkling sketches and dialogues and his skillful adaptations of French comedies portended genuine playwriting talent. Molnár readily accepted the challenge and most of all the 200 *Korona* advance (his monthly salary at the paper was exactly half). But by the time he was putting the finishing touches to his play, *A doctor úr*, Beőthy resigned and left for Paris. Unperturbed, Molnár submitted the script to the Vigszinház (Comedy Theater) instead, which accepted it at once.[6] As a consequence of his "default," he had to wait for fourteen years before any of his plays could be presented at the National Theater, but he became the "house-author" of the Comedy Theater. The premiere took place on November 28, 1902. The play was a notable success; it had thirty performances, an extraordinary feat at that time in a Budapest repertory theater.

The title, *A doctor úr* (The Lawyer), did not refer to a physician but an attorney. In Hungary lawyers had to earn a doctorate, *doctor juris*, hence the English title, *The Lawyer*. Though it is included in *APM*, this hilarious farce was never produced in English.

The play's central character is an altruistic petty criminal, Puzsér, who repeatedly steals and robs so that his lawyer friend, Dr. Sárkány, may have a practice and earn a professional reputation defending him. Together they stage ingenious break-ins. This time, the scheme is to change clothes and identities: Puzsér will pose as Sárkány at a high-school reunion—"old classmates don't remember faces"—while his partner will steal all available valuables in his own home during the night. If Sárkány, disguised as Puzsér, is caught, he would be identified by his family and pretend it was a joke. But things go haywire. The "thief" is spotted by a policeman and pandemonium ensues. At the dramatic moment, each member of the household is engaged in various clandestine, illegal activities. Mrs. Sárkány, a bored, flirtatious woman, is seeing her lover, none other than the chief of police; her young sister, who boards with them, is planning a secret marriage with Sárkány's clerk; the prudish governess is plotting against everyone. In the mass confusion, after Sárkány is arrested, Puzsér arrives as an "outraged attorney" and takes command. In the end the lawyer is released and forgives his wife, the young couple receives the family's consent, the generous Puzsér vows to "help" his friend again, and as he exits he sanctimoniously blesses them all.

This preposterous situation comedy, fashioned after the popular French models, contained all the elements of a good farce—misunderstanding, confusion, deception, contrast, surprise, fast dialogue, and grotesque movements—all designed only to provoke laughter. Though character portrayal was rather perfunctory and scenes were heaped upon one another ponderously, the author confidently manipulated the complex plot. Molnár seemed well versed in stage technique; his timing was perfect, and both the cleverly calculated effects and the glib dialogue with associative verbal wit showed that he was a born theatrical craftsman, just as Beőthy had suspected.

The idea for the plot might have come to Molnár from Tristan Bernard's plays. In 1898, when he began writing *The Lawyer*, Molnár was translating Bernard's plays and had seen the Parisian performance of *The Only Bandit of the Village*. It features a lawyer who catches a thief, believing him to be his wife's lover. Similar conflict occurs in *The Gang at Leon*, in which a husband mistakes his wife's lover for a thief.

This first play introduced Molnár's favorite future themes: "love conquers all," marital problems, reversed identities; it also launched his innate character types: middle-aged, jealous husband; frivolous, crafty wife; innocent young lovers; and shrewd servants. Both the audience and the critics welcomed the fresh new voice; the pioneer work of the twenty-four-year-old playwright was greeted as a stage sensation. One contemporary review commented: "Our anticipations were highly rewarded; the young Molnár might become Hungary's leading comedy writer. His brilliant dialogues, puns and quick mastery of the mechanics indeed forecast a promising artist. If he does not get spoiled by success and develops his craft, matures and pays more attention to structure, some day we may all be mighty proud of him."[7] How prophetic this commentary proved to be!

In the following years Molnár adapted four French comedies. This labor earned him money but brought no satisfaction. He had to decide whether he could find his own dramatic voice or remain content with imitating foreign masters—a lucrative but

unimaginative road to fame. Soon he decided to write another
farce based on his popular newspaper sketches, featuring the
overpampered *enfant terrible* Józsi, whose preoccupation was
teasing and blackmailing the adult world. The play *Józsi* opened
in January 1904. Never translated into English, it was published
in Molnár's *Összes Művei* (Collected Works) in Hungarian.[8]

The plotline is extremely complicated and the cast is enormous, including more than a dozen main characters. Mrs.
Csongrády, at odds with her husband, is in love with Dr. Verpeléti, who is about to marry Widow Tóth. To prevent the
nuptials, the devious lady summons one of her admirers, Sebő,
a notorious "Don Juan," to compromise Mrs. Tóth. He is to
appear at the Tóth's summer resort when the suitor arrives. To
supervise the happenings, Mrs. Csongrády rents the villa next
door. Mrs. Tóth has several houseguests, among them her
nephew Józsi and "Uncle" Lajos, the late Mr. Tóth's best friend.
Lajos has also been recruited to the conspiracy since he had
promised Tóth never to let his widow remarry. The stage is
set, all are in readiness, but Józsi, sneaking around both households, is privy to all secrets. He blackmails everyone and in
the crucial moment disrupts the well orchestrated act, spoils
all the plans by his mere presence and by "innocently" revealing each character's machinations. In one chaotic moment a
woman cries "Józsi is to blame for all the mess!" But it all
ends well: the Csongrádys make up, Dr. Verpeléti marries the
happy widow, Sebő escapes, and all the young lovers unite
in bliss. Józsi only grins and counts his bribe money contentedly.

The play, somewhat reminiscent of *The Lawyer*, was written
again in typical farce tradition: husbands and wives, fiancés and
lovers rush in and out, finding each other in the most compro-
mising situations. Molnár's humor is irresistible; the dialogue
is vibrant and quick, adorned with puns and bons mots. In burlesque manner, one comic scene rapidly follows another. The
unexpected, meticulously timed twists are juggled with slap-
stick technique evoking riotous laughter. But the play lacks
unity; it is overcrowded and overcomplicated. Some parts are
sloppy and the language often slips into uncouth colloquialism.
Nevertheless, Molnár's dramatic acumen is apparent and his
portrayal of Józsi proves again his keen insight into a child's

psyche. The general characterization shows noticeable improvement. The chief manipulator, Mrs. Csongrády, is especially effective; like a puppeteer pulling strings, she cynically plays with people's lives and foreshadows her male counterpart, the Devil, in Molnár's next play.

These first two comedies in themselves bore no particular significance, but the effect of their success on the playwright was incalculable. He became self-confident, acquainted himself with the stage and its paraphernalia, learned about audience psychology, and, most of all, earned a name as a playwright.

III World Success: The Devil

Following the presentation of *Józsi,* Molnár continued his journalistic work, wrote novels, and searched for material for a new comic play. Once, after having seen the performance of *Faust,* he hit on the notion that it might be amusing to present Mephisto as a seemingly ordinary man, making him both a protagonist in a comedy of sex and a symbol of evil desire in each character. To feature the omnipotent devil amid sexual intrigue would appeal to the public, Molnár contended, since in those days philandering was a kind of civic status in Budapest, and "Satan as a dramatic device would ridicule the jealous and titillate the curious."[9] Struck by the idea, he began writing *Az ördög* (The Devil) while staying in a hotel on Margaret Island. (He was already separated from his first wife at this time.) Four months later, on April 10, 1907, the play opened at the Comedy Theater and was an instant success, earning the author membership into the exclusive Petőfi Society. But it would have been soon forgotten had it not been for an unexpected turn of events.

Toward the end of the season, Ermete Zacconi, the noted Italian actor-manager accidentally saw a performance of *The Devil.* This event proved mutually serendipitous: Zacconi landed his most successful play and a favorite role—he played the part of the Devil intermittently for thirty years—and Molnár became an international playwright. The sensational Turin premiere was a theatrical milestone, as it attracted most of the European stage dignitaries. Understandably, the news spread and a few months later the play opened in Berlin, and soon after in practically every capital of Europe.

New York managers frantically fought for production rights, and hurried translations were prepared. In August 1908, two American productions of *The Devil* opened simultaneously—an unprecedented event in Broadway's history.[10] Shortly afterwards the play was also running in New York's Yiddish and German theaters. Within a year it was produced in forty-three languages. In the United States alone, at the height of the season one reviewer estimated that "no less than thirty companies were staging the play."[11]

Both English versions ran in triumph. One, adapted by William Trowbridge Larned, starred George Arliss; the other, by Oliver Herford, had Edwin Stevens in the leading role. Neither of the two renditions was completely faithful to the original. The Herford version, translated from a German script, transplanted the locale to Vienna and gave German names to the characters. The Larned version retained the Budapest setting but made frequent changes in the dialogue.[12] We shall cite the Herford text, the subsequently authorized English script.

The story concerns Olga Zanden, the pretty young wife of an elderly jealous banker (a stock odious husband of the period), and Karl, a painter. The two of them were in love years ago. Now Zanden, a pretentious parvenu, unaware of the inflammable situation, brings his wife to the studio of the by now fashionable artist and insists on his painting her in the décolleté. Then he departs. The couple discuss their old romance with nostalgia. When she remains alone, shy and hesitant to undress for the posing, the Devil appears from nowhere, wearing a tuxedo, calling himself Mr. Miller—Molnár's name in English. He expounds his "immoral moralities" in long speeches. Soon Karl returns and the couple notice a gradual intensification of their rekindled love. Later, the omnipresent Miller, through various tricks, breaks up the relationship between Karl and his former fiancée and manipulates the circumstances that make Olga's final yielding to adultery very convenient. The young lovers keep resisting his temptation by exercising restraint and by seeking other means to stay virtuous. Olga selects a rich heiress to marry Karl, hoping that "an uninspired marriage will be safer than a thrilling but hazardous affair" (74). The artist, on the other hand, "cools his passion" with his earthy model, Mimi. But the Devil is persistent. With ostensible cynicism he prompts Olga to send Karl a love letter—which he dictates—promising submission, and volunteers its safe delivery. He seems to comply when, a bit later, she bids him to destroy it; but when, vacillating, she wishes it back, he produced the epistle unharmed, declaring that he burned a tailor's bill instead. Olga snatches the letter, which proves her passionate asseveration and also seals her fate. As she goes to join the painter, the Devil triumphantly rubs his hands, points at the bedroom door, smiling diabolically, and says, "Voilà!" Then the curtain falls.

All that happened was little enough: a devious Mephisto forced two young people together who might have remained virtuous without him. The play's importance lies not in its plot but in its themes. In *The Devil*, Molnár launches his theories about women, about their relationship with men, and jealousy, topics he would expand in endless variations in his subsequent plays, novels, and short stories. His female characters are travesties of Shaw's "life force": cunning, unfathomable, fickle, and illogical. At one point the Devil states: "If women wrote timetables, they would tell all the hours at which trains did not start, and all the places at which you must not stop to get to your destination" (85). Men are presented as their victims, forever intrigued, baffled, and, ultimately, defeated by women. Even the Devil admits men's inferiority when he says, "We are indeed the weaker sex" (75).

The introduction of a negative supernatural element is also partly related to the psychology of relative truth applied to women. But it goes beyond that. From his first inexplicable entrance when he utters: "I am one who always comes at the right moment—I come from Nowhere" (62), the Devil establishes himself as a flesh-and-blood personality intimately acquainted with everyone. He emerges as a variation of the gnostic Prince of Darkness, a polite, sophisticated go-between, anticipating people's thoughts, controlling their actions, and breaking their inhibitions. As a protagonist of duplicity, temptation, and malignancy he becomes the symbol of people's dual personality; in Jungian terms, our "shadow," or the Freudian

"Id." Thus, the play can be interpreted as an allegorical study of evil instincts in mankind. However, Molnár's Satan lacks the seriousness of Goethe's Mephistopheles or the Romantic significance of other literary Lucifers. No scheming villain but rather an "Uncle Devil," he is a glib, cynical, seamy demon conjured up by the collective unconscious of the people involved. The play's thematic aim is to make the Devil represent only the hidden impulses of true passion which often seem to be at war with social exaction.

By revealing the dominance of hypocrisy and pretense, he also intends to teach a lesson. The implicit symbolism in his character, however, raises the comedy above its somewhat ordinary satire of social conventions. In one of his speeches, the Devil outlines his (or Molnár's) basic philosophy:

The only end of life is to burn—to burn yourself up. You must flame and blaze like a torch and toss the fire about you. I know! Your moralist will tell you to love one another—don't believe them—your grubby little earth with its paltry million years is not ripe for such love as that. It can only breed monks, madmen or Methodists. Don't be a rogue but a jolly rogue and the world is yours! Look at me! I own the earth. Here is the key to life—live yourself—only yourself. . . . Kiss the sweetest lips, drink the wine of Life—Drink! Drink! Drink! Drink! (64)

The characterization is subtle and colorful; Olga, the unpredictable, crafty woman epitomizing all the qualities of her bourgeois sisters; Mimi, the penniless, sophisticated, sensuous temptress, kin to those millions of basically decent but poor girls who are compelled to sell their bodies for bread; and Elsa, the powerful heiress whose hauteur and pretense are upheld by wealth . . . individually represent various aspects of the composite Molnáresque feminine stereotype. The male partners, Karl and Zanden, come alive as naive, unsuspecting men easily outwitted by the "Women."

The language, inventive and witty, shows a strong influence of Oscar Wilde. The Devil's monologues are richly adorned with epigrams and paradoxes: "The real wife, always another man's wife, of course, is like a single eyeglass—it looks very nice but one's better off without it" (63). Unfortunately, because of several untranslatable Hungarian idioms, parts have been deleted and some English lines merely imply the original meaning or remain obscure.

The Devil established Molnár as the first Hungarian playwright to become internationally known and marked the beginning of his rising fame. After 1907, the theatrical managers of Europe and overseas never failed to attend the premieres of his plays.

IV *Satires of Marriage:* The Guardsman *and* The Wolf

Around 1908, Molnár's career was foiled by contradictions. His artistic success was marred by domestic calamities, which, in turn, offered subjects for his creations. In 1908, after his first wife, Margit Vészi, left him, Molnár was harassed by scurrilous gossip about his sadistic, cruel treatment of women. Overcome by guilt and disgust, he found comfort in transmitting his inner conflicts into dramatic art. By 1909, he completed his masterpiece *Liliom*, in which he exorcised himself through immortalizing his "lost" wife, in Juli's role. Ironically, however, during the play's rehearsal he fell in love with Irén Varsányi, the actress playing the part. Their subsequent scandalous love affair and its entanglements provided the plots for his next two plays. In these social comedies the playwright hurled his dramatic javelin at stale marriages and jealous husbands, which were ideal satiric targets, as well as sobering facts he himself had to contend with in reality.

A testőr (The Guardsman), a sparkling comedy of adult sophistication, written for and about his lover, opened in 1910 at the Comedy Theater. It was an instant hit: there were twenty-five curtain calls at the Budapest premiere. But the play's first English presentation, entitled *Where Ignorance Is Bliss*, failed on Broadway in 1913 and closed after eight performances.[13] Eleven years later, a new adaptation by Philip Moeller, bearing the original title, *The Guardsman*, starring Alfred Lunt and Lynn Fontanne, achieved an enormous popular success and ran 248 times. Since 1924, the Moeller version has been the accepted text.

The story concerns a talented, insanely jealous actor and his lovely wife, a famous actress, also known for her frequent, much-publicized liaisons. She is now playing Chopin on the piano, a sure sign of her yearning for a new romance after six months of marriage. The husband has reason to believe that her fancy has been caught by a Russian guardsman. Convinced of his superior acting ability, the desperate actor plans an intricate test of her fidelity: utilizing his histrionic powers to impersonate the guard, he sets out to seduce his own wife. The action of the play turns on the carrying out of this enterprise. He pretends to leave for a guest performance but actually disguises himself and reappears as a glittering guardsman. He pursues the tactics of a lover, hoping that he will be rebuffed. But the actress, rather, encourages his attention. That night he flirts with her in the proscenium box at the opera, obtains a passionate kiss and an invitation for a date. After this the actor is loath to persist in his deceit. The following day he arrives back "unexpectedly" in his own person, ready for a showdown. But she ridicules him, professing that she knew his identity from the onset and merely played her part "to fool him." The husband thus has to choose between wounding his professional pride and the loss of faith in his wife. The play ends on a note of doubt and a touch of cynicism.

ACTOR.   If you knew why didn't you tell me from the beginning?
ACTRESS. Because I wanted you to play the comedy out to the end. I certainly didn't think you'd lack the courage to go through with it. I didn't think you'd rob us of that beautiful night. (181)

When the curtain falls, the actress is again demurely playing Chopin, as in the opening scene.

This pungent, frivolous comedy, an apotheosis of jealousy, presents the predicament of a man who feels he is not loved for what he thinks he is and needs to masquerade as what he believes his wife wants. Since he schemed not only to prove himself as a man but to demonstrate his acting ability, he traps himself into a compromise no matter how she reacts. The critic warns him: "It looks bad, my friend, she's in love with you as a guardsman. You won't be able to control yourself—you'll seduce your own wife" (169). And he almost does. Except that the wife is also masquerading, pretending to be ignorant of the guard's identity, only to reveal at the end that her responses were also only play-acting to prove her worth as an actress. Thus, the actor's self-revelation is voided of meaning by his wife's pretense of pretense.

Molnár contrasted relative and absolute truths before Pirandello. He did not deal simply in lies; he dealt in illusions of the truth that are made true only because people believe in them. The opposing characters are right because there is really no way of establishing where the forever elusive reality and truth may lie hidden. In *The Guardsman* no truth can be known, only verisimilitude. The bait of appearances masks the hook of reality, but the mysterious "fish" of honest life is never caught and perhaps never can be since both "fishermen" are born artists of pretense by the virtue of their profession. As Molnár views it, man is forever involved in futile illusions and an obsessive quest to know the unknowable "truth."[14] Showing the relationship between surface and essence later becomes one of Molnár's most favored themes, and "stage folks" his pet *dramatis personae.*

In this play, the author created a theater-within-the-theater and produced a supreme form of the art of make-believe, by venturing a most improbable encounter between a couple. When people told Molnár that it was unlikely that a woman would fail to recognize her own husband no matter how ingenious the vocal and physical disguise, he dismissed the argument: "The theater exists to lie—except in essentials. If the audience will accept a painted canvas as a forest, they'll accept this. They'll believe she didn't recognize him because *I* say she didn't."[15] As it were, the couple's flamboyant artificiality seemed absolutely right for a play that seemingly equated marriage with a theatrical performance and encumbered their private lives with more stage contrivances than they would ever encounter in the roles of Othello and Desdemona.

One of the contemporary critics, Ignotus, reviewing the Hungarian premiere stated that this play was like a refined, high-class chess game "except the pawns and kings are live peo-

ple. . . . Molnár is a conductor of the theatrical orchestra: the
audience, the actors, and the stage are his instruments. His new
play is a dazzling dramatic bravura."[16]
The style is gracious and poetic; Molnár tosses off his thin
and perilously unbelievable story with great ease. The con-
spiratory tone, interwoven with irony, lends the play an urbane
sophistication. The dialogues are swift and full of sanguine
exuberance even when dispersing Molnár's philosophy. By leaving the couple nameless instead of individualizing the characters, the author underlines his satiric intent and projects a
universal image. George Bernard Shaw's prediction that this
play would endure with the finest works of modern playwriting
has proven to be correct: *The Guardsman* is still a popular play
of repertory theaters all over the world.

Two years elapsed before another Molnár play saw the boards.
A farkas (The Wolf) premiered in 1912 at the Magyar Szinház
(Hungarian Theater). This pseudo-Freudian dream-play, ex-
ploring the workings of the unconscious, had much in common
with *The Devil* and *The Guardsman*; in fact, it attacked the
same problems from different angles. With the portrayal of
Irén Varsányi and her possessive husband, Molnár paid a last
tribute to the memory of his great love. In America there were
two versions again: the first, presented as *The Phantom Rival*
in Leo Ditrichstein's adaptation, opened to rave reviews on
Broadway in 1914; the second, a much more accurate translation by Melville Baker entitled *The Tale of the Wolf*, closed
after thirteen performances during the 1925–26 season.[17] In
our discussion we shall cite the later version, published in *APM*.

The body of the play is a dream. Kelemen, a middle-aged
Budapest lawyer lacking charm and Romantic glamour, drives
his wife, Vilma, to near hysteria with his constant jealous nag-
ging. At the opening of the play, his suspicion is inflamed at a
restaurant by the appearance of Vilma's first love, Szabó. Late
that night she rereads Szabó's old love letters, written seven
years ago when he left to become famous and rich. He vowed
to remain true to her through all vicissitudes and, after reaching a brilliant career, come back to claim her. She falls asleep
and dreams of her lover's return in different roles: as a decorated colonel, a charismatic diplomat, a celebrated singer, and

finally, as a virile lackey. She is always willing to join her suitor and each time their escape is thwarted by some monstrous meddler: husband, mother, or friends. Each incident is played with extravagance by her mythical heroes, but by her, with a sentiment that belongs to the dream. Although Kelemen is not totally absent, his jealousy is less obtrusive. When she awakens in rapture, normal life resumes. It so happens that her husband is dealing with an investment firm that sends over a clerk who turns out to be Szabó. In real life her built-up idol is a poor, dull, spineless alcoholic. The encounter helps her to get rid of her illusions. Kelemen wins new confidence as a husband and Vilma returns to her domestic responsibilities.

The symbolic title refers to the familiar "Tale of the Wolf" Vilma is wont to tell her son as a bedtime story but never finishes before the child falls asleep. In the end, Kelemen finally concludes the story that proves only a bugaboo. Husbands are like the people who cry "wolf"; for them, the danger lies not in reality but in the perfervid fancy of their romantic wives. Confront these women with reality and the phantom rivals vanish at once. According to Molnár, every woman carries the memory of her first love, whom she has glorified into an ideal by which she measures her husband.

In 1912 the play appeared rather inventive, especially in its stage technique. To stage Vilma's subconscious somewhat in the same manner as Willy Loman's daydreams are staged later in Miller's *Death of a Salesman* was indeed an ingenious design. Molnár used several other artistic and psychological devices to create a "credible" illusion. During the transformation, no curtain is lowered; in the darkness only a dim light flickers, gradually getting brighter, then, in a shaft of illumination, the imaginary warrior emerges resplendent in a uniform of rank. The absurdly abrupt transition from one lover to another takes place on stage in the dark. Each Szabó uses slightly exaggerated rhetoric and, concurrent with the way the unconscious mind works, there are occasional incoherent passages in the dialogues. Finally a servant's knock on the door breaks the illusion when both the dream and the scene revert back to reality with normal lighting. In contrast with the rather banal plot, Molnár maintains a seriousness of temperament and intensity of purpose and thus attains the high velocity of the comic. The language and the tempo alter with the changes: in the fantasy scene the style is more formalized, filled with pathos, lingering and halting, enhancing the impression of the heroine's dreamlike helplessness. When Vilma talks to her lovers in simplistic, interrupted phrases: "Ah, my glorious hero! I die for love of you!—I was untrue to you—but my heart is yours—Believe that . . . and go! Leave me to atone" (210), it sounds like those "oldies" on television dotted with charmingly preposterous lines. When the final awakening approaches, the rhythm quickens and the language gains concreteness.

VILMA.   Poor boy!
LACKEY. Don't pity me!
VILMA.   I am yours!
LACKEY. You lie.
VILMA.   Forever!
LACKEY. You lie!
VILMA.   I am not lying.
LACKEY. Then . . .
VILMA.   Then?
LACKEY. Kiss me! You beautiful, faithless, noble lady! (225)

Molnár's irrepressible irony, cynicism, and the satiric undertone save the play from becoming a melodrama.

Thematically the play's importance lies in its Freudian approach, a rather daring dramatic device in 1912. Molnár first experimented with psychoanalytical techniques (or tricks) in *The Devil*, and now he continued to apply the same formula. This trend later became his unique dramatic approach. In accordance with his subliminal distrust of women, Molnár wrote numerous variations on the theme of feminine duplicity, elaborating on woman's primordial desire to corrupt and seduce men. But in the crucial moment of exigency, his heroines were usually stopped by the warning of the Super-Ego—the rational mind—and tragic falls were averted, tension was eased, and the conflicts were resolved in comic relief. *The Wolf* was a typical example of the author's half-serious treatment of women in his comedies. By crystallizing the wishful, romantic daydreams of a bored wife into scenes in which reality and fancy, conscious and unconscious yearnings were piquantly mingled, Molnár created a facile and entertaining, albeit dated, drama.

V *Plays during World War I*: The White Cloud, Carnival, Fashions for Men

During 1914–15 Molnár worked as a war correspondent at the Galician front. Surrounded by the horrors of destruction, he wrote his next drama, *A fehér felhő* (The White Cloud) at military headquarters. This brief, pathos-ridden miracle play, one of his weakest pieces, opened in 1916 at the National Theater and won him the Voinits Prize, the Hungarian Academy's most distinguished award. The country's conservative leadership exploited the play's emotional impact and used it as propaganda material to rekindle ebbing patriotic sentiments. It has never been produced in America, but Louis Rittenberg, editor of *APM*, included his translation of the play in the collection.

The short first scene is a reenactment of an icy December night on the Galician front, strewn by corpses. Soldiers are singing in the trenches and muffled cannon shots are heard as the General listens to the report about the latest casualties: ninety-four hussars killed. Scene two takes place in a tiny agricultural village in Hungary and shows the effect the news has upon their families. The almost-illiterate, work-weary wives, resigned to the "inevitable," share their sorrows with one another and try to comfort the children by telling them that "all hussars, the glorious heroes, go up to the white cloud when they die . . . there you'll meet your fathers again" (243). The youngsters, obsessed by this idea, climb the nearby mountain determined to visit their fathers. The rest of the play continues on the cloud—in heaven—where the dead hussars are seen thronging around an angel. This celestial commandant conducts an odd interrogation: "Was it really necessary that you die? . . . Fighting for what? For Whom? Why such supreme heroism?" One bloody figure replies: "Little Angel, it's so easy to ask but oh so very hard to answer" (248).

When the Angel announces the children's visit, the fathers begin worrying about their appearance: the shabby, blood-soaked uniforms, rusty swords, and bare feet would hardly fit their image. But when the children arrive a miracle occurs: amidst thunder and red lightning, they find themselves on white stallions, wearing glittering capes of pure gold braided with diamonds, and waving shiny swords. Thus the myth is confirmed and their image remains intact. The awkward reunion takes place in pantomime. After each child has found his own father, the couples start for a walk while the other hussars present them with gold coins and flowers: "Let them tell it to the village as they saw it here. Let the hussar go on being a hussar" (259). The last scene flashes up the battlefield as in the first scene with suspended figures; only shots, sounding like salvos, and distant, melancholy singing are audible.

Here Molnár again used psychology to demonstrate how legends are created and destroyed. His attack was aimed at those who cynically manipulated the archetypal hero myth. The heavenly interrogation revealed that the brave hussars "had been herded to death like sheep, used as sacrificial lambs" (249). These simple patriots starved, froze, and suffered for a cause they could not even comprehend but, since their superiors "guaranteed" heavenly rewards, they fought bravely and died to live up to their mythical reputation. The playwright obviously intended to satirize sham heroics and criticize war-mongers, along with politicians who had promoted and hailed the senseless manslaughter under the slogan of patriotic duty. Nonetheless, Molnár's noble intentions were thwarted. The play's imminent bitter irony was misconstrued and its theme was not interpreted as a repudiation of war but as a poetic requiem dedicated to the memory of the Hungarian hussars' majestic sacrifices for their country.

The play's effectiveness was meant to be heightened by the supernatural elements, a dramatic device the author had already used, but the encounter in heaven conveyed nothing more than sentimentality, a tear-jerking gimmick that reduced the action to sugar-coated, heartrending melodrama. Such a flatulent scene with starry-eyed children promenading on white clouds, accompanied by glamorous, fairy-tale-like warriors and majestic angels, could appeal only to a naive, undemanding audience "overdoped" by bombastic propaganda.

The original play was written in a dialect used in a certain Hungarian province. In the extremely poor and inaccurate translation the primitive hussars, their wives and children speak pidgin English, using broken phrases and ungrammatical sentences. To match their excessive simplicity, even the Angel condescends and talks haltingly, spelling out each word as if the characters were feeble-minded: "Children, did you say? Oh! . . . Didn't I tell you? . . . Oh, inquisitive angel that I am . . . here now, I keep talking. . . . While I should be telling you. . . . Listen! Why . . . this is the news I have for you, good hussars—the children, yours are coming" (251).

Technically, the play offered nothing new although the transition from reality to the transcendental spheres took place in a most fantastic manner. As the panic-stricken mothers reach out to pull their children back from the cliff, the youngsters suddenly disappear; glaring lights blind the women and "organ music blurts into crescendo as they all look petrified heavenward" (246). To stage such a scene and remain credible was no easy feat for a director. Voinits Prize notwithstanding, Molnár seldom talked about *The White Cloud* which, by most critics, was regarded as "the poorest, most atypical and inferior of his plays of the period."[18]

After his return from the front, to relax from the tension of war, Molnár wrote a symbolic social comedy, *Farsang* (Carnival), which opened at the Comedy Theater in 1916 to mixed reception.[19] Its English adaptation by Melville Baker, though staged eight years later on Broadway, drew similar, mostly unfavorable criticism and closed after thirteen performances.

Molnár designed the play for the benefit of his new lover, Sári Fedák, a celebrated diva. Determined that she should become an actress, the playwright featured her as the play's tragicomic leading lady. Thanks to this piece, Fedák did change from a prima donna to a theatrical star and played the heroine in several subsequent Molnár dramas.

The story unfolds in a grand ballroom in Budapest toward the end of the nineteenth century. Every year the lovely Camilla Oroszy and her elderly, tyrannical husband, a nobleman, leave their country estate to attend the social activities during the carnival season. The young heroine, an exuberant, outdoor person, is utterly bored with her life-style and eagerly awaits someone to awaken her intellectually and emotionally. In the capital, she is besieged by admirers whom she finds stupid except for one poetic idler, Nikolaus, who professes to have loved her for years. At the ball an unexpected event puts into her hands a means of testing his devotion and of fleeing from domestic thralldom. Camilla stumbles across a priceless stone lost from the Princess's crown and conceals it, not from avarice but as a symbol of power. While court officials search the place for the jewel, she challenges Nikolaus to escape with her and the glittering bauble. But the young man does not measure up to such abandon. Why sacrifice comfort and respectability? Instead, he suggests divorce or a clandestine romance. Camilla then realizes that her hero has no courage to be "natural," and tosses the gem on the floor, where the police find it. She surrenders the timid, "hypocritical" admirer to another lady guest and departs with her gruff, jealous husband "like a dead woman," to be shackled again with the chains of marital tyranny. The carnival is over. Camilla has been awakened, but only to learn that her dream was better.

This lightweight psychological study, seemingly modeled after *Madame Bovary* without its depth and universality, failed for several reasons. First of all, the author could not realize the inherent possibilities of his theme. While reiterating the basic premise of *The Wolf*, Molnár went a step further. Previously the heroines were the ones unwilling to give up wealth and security for love; they merely flirted or played with fire. Camilla, however, was less romantic and more resolute; she wanted all or nothing, and it was her lover who refused to make the sacrifice. In this new situation, however, the heroine appeared totally unconvincing.

In the English translation Molnár's social message, too, was lost. Camilla's motivating forces and the environment in which she challenged love could not be completely understood without an appreciation of the original setting. Without comprehension of the social and historical background of Hungary in the 1850s, the story was implausible. The original text gave resonance to the country's mood: after the defeat of the 1848 Revolution revulsion for the Monarchy was widespread in Hungary, especially among the gentry. Camilla's repeated outburst clearly echoed her people's anti-Austrian sentiments: "I despise the whole scene with Her Highness! Why does the Austrian Royal Family come here to sparkle—why do they stir up the ordinary citizens?" (263). Even the lost jewel symbolizes more than a token of her temporary power; it served as a symbol of her revolt against high society's unabashed admiration for the court. Furthermore, among the refined, perfumed aristocratic dandies, Oroszy's crude naturalness, her preference for gypsy music rather than the opera, for the circus rather than the theater, were intended as expressions of the Hungarian national spirit seeking to develop its own culture rather than imitating foreign conventions. Unfortunately, little of this essential material came through in the adaptation. Also, in the English version the time was set not as the 1850s but "the turn of the century," when social and political conditions were entirely different. By specifying the time, Molnár provided a vantage point from which the play could be judged not only historically but dramatically as well. In the *fin de siècle* milieu much of the English dialogue sounded shallow, wearisome, and inane and the conversations failed to reverberate the mood of the decadent "salon period" recreated in the original play. The playwright deliberately used artificial sentences to match the powdered fops who uttered them. Since Molnár's stylistic intentions were overlooked, the play indeed sounded forced and archaic.

Carnival was intended as a minidrama transpiring in the heroine's psyche, a fictive attempt to change an entire life within an hour; instead, it became a maxikitsch, a mediocre comedy of manners. Understandably, neither Hungary during the bloody war years nor America in the Roaring Twenties could be intrigued by this type of entertainment.

Molnár's next play, *Úridivat* (Fashions for Men), a farcical comedy of character, was somewhat more successful. It opened at the National Theater in 1917 to enthusiastic reception. The Broadway public, however, failed to respond in similar vein to Benjamin Glazer's adaptation, despite the critical acclaim and the fact that the play ran simultaneously in two theaters during the 1922–23 season.[20]

In the aimlessly drifting plot the interest lies primarily in establishing the main character's personality. Péter Juhász, the humble proprietor of a haberdashery, is a modern-day saint, a noble altruist who will hear no evil, speak no evil, see no evil. Spending all his time in the shop, he tirelessly caters to the often-outrageous tastes of his clientele and to the whims of his family and employees. Business goes fairly well until his wife embezzles a large sum of money, steals their savings, and runs away with Oscar, the store's star salesman. Instead of being incensed, the double-crossed husband reacts with self-abasement and compassion for the rascal and his devious wife, even when he learns that his business went bankrupt. Péter then accepts a post as a director of cheese production on the estate of his benefactor, the Count. His ambitious young accountant, Paula, accompanies him there, ostensibly in a gesture of loyalty but actually with the intent of becoming "His Excellency's" mistress. On the farm, impositions on Péter's saintliness multiply, but his spirit of love and kindness drives him on. He assumes the role of both Paula's chaperone and guardian angel of the husbandry. No sacrifice is too great for him to preserve her virtue and to satisfy his laborers. While pestering his boss with vigilance, Péter falls in love with his "ward" and eventually takes her back to Budapest. In the last scene, as the future Mrs. Juhász, Paula takes over as cashier in the repossessed haberdashery.

Molnár's theme develops an almost biblical notion, namely, that generous innocence ultimately conquers guile and that if one is noble others will follow suit. This message is conveyed through his naive, Job-like hero, who elicits both admiration and exasperation. A pure Parsifal without medieval trappings, he is referred to as St. Francis of Assisi and Dostoevsky's idiot, Prince Mishkin. But he is much more reminiscent of Dekker's subservient linen draper in *The Honest Whore*, who, in a similar manner, endures any insolence from his customers and endless provocation from his contemptuous spouse. With character delineation edging on caricature, Molnár's hero comes across as a satire on the meek variety of the male sex rather than a modern saint or a "holy fool." Péter's idealism, impracticality, limitless capacity for sacrifice, and unwarranted trust of mankind seem so exaggerated that the play shifts into farce. Therefore, since his blind goodness and selfless deeds border on benevolent idiocy, in our time he can only be regarded as a pitiful yet spurious comic hero.

Despite, or perhaps because of, this ambiguity, the American critics deemed the play's characterization "incomparably fresh," Péter's self-limited virtues "genuinely convincing," and claimed that "Molnár presented his comedy of sainthood with an art of realism as finely true as the art of *Liliom*."[21] We may disagree, but the Hungarian reviewers also sounded quite impressed by the play. According to Krúdy, "this comedy gave a lesson about honesty, decency, and generosity to the sinful capital and its mortal twist touched the heart of even the super-cynics. Molnár manipulated the audience like a trickster with hypnotic power and made beards tremble both with fury and emotions."[22]

In the original the dialogues are lithe and graceful. Part of the play's humor lies in the contrast between the overly polite shopkeeper's flowery language and the colloquial tongue used by his customers. Molnár exploits, to fine comic effect, the social discriminations, with their corresponding usages and honorifics, of the old Budapest society. In fact, Péter is further encumbered by these formulas of abject deference. His schooled patience and self-effacing diffidence serve to emphasize class consciousness as well as to enhance characterization. But many of these phrases lose significance in English, where one is addressed (if at all) as "Sir" or "Madam" and not as "your excellency" or "your honor."

The action moves swiftly despite the play's uncharacteristic lack of structure. Some of the minor characters are extremely amusing, among them Philip, the drudge, who has seen the last act of *Lohengrin* sixteen times, but has never been able to leave the shop early enough to behold the swan's entrance; or the cunning drunkard, Máté, a hired man at the estate, who, with crude tricks, dupes Péter into any wage-raise he wants. Molnár also utilizes adroitly the inherent comic elements of the setting, both in the world of lisle-socks and jockey-caps and the Count's bucolic manor redolent of cheese.

Now, the play appears stilted and dated. Edmund Wilson aptly explains why *Fashions for Men*, a play he called "a comic masterpiece," fails to appeal in our time: "A gentle shopkeeper who allows himself to be swindled by his wife and his assistant, who emerges as a saint with the love of his once discontent but later adoring cashier, to return to his Heaven-sent vocation, could hardly be tolerated as a hero nowadays."[23]

VI   Romances among Aristocrats and Stage-Folks:
The Swan and Theatre

The extremely vain playwright was so insulted by occasional criticisms that he wrote nothing for the stage for three years. His first postwar play, A hattyú (The Swan), a beguiling Romantic comedy, which opened at the Comedy Theater in 1920, proved to be a felicitous launching of the new decade that was to witness the apex of Molnár's dramatic career. This wistful poetic romance completely mesmerized both the Budapest audience and, shortly afterwards, the entire theatrical world. In New York the play became an instant box-office hit and a bestseller in 1923.[24] The rapturous reception in America was all the more amazing because the play dealt with love and jealousy in an aristocratic milieu, and reveling in royal tradition or watching the mechanics of dynastic marriages was hardly the favorite pastime of New Yorkers during the Flapper Era. Nonetheless, Molnár's magic worked: the play's artistry, skill, and imagination captured the public, which, as one critic reported, "applauded a brilliant performance with a spontaneity and intensity of enthusiasm seldom surpassed in our theatre."[25]

The play is set at a castle in an imaginary kingdom where Princess Beatrice, widow of a deposed house, is anxious to restore the family hegemony through the marriage of her daughter, Alexandra, to Prince Albert, heir apparent to the throne. To this end the energetic royal mother has invited the crown prince for a visit. The pretty young princess consents to sacrifice herself for the exaltation of her house, but Albert, a boorish fellow, remains maddeningly indifferent. Then the impatient mother has an inspiration: she will prod the man to action by making him jealous. The target is Nicholaus Ági, the tutor who secretly worships Alexandra. She reluctantly lends herself to her mother's scheme and invites the young scholar to the royal banquet as a decoy. Ági, overwhelmed by Alexandra's sudden attention, boldly declares his long-suppressed adoration and sweeps the princess into the passionate experience of first love. In dreamy ecstasy, he grows assertive and insults his "rival" whose jealousy is now sufficiently aroused. Irritated, Albert ridicules the tutor with contempt, but when he is about to smack "the insolent commoner," Alexandra comes forward and, in front of all the guests, suddenly hugs and kisses her humiliated friend. Apparently the royal match is ruined. The mother faints and total confusion follows until Father Hyacinth, Alexandra's jovial uncle, saves the day. The wise priest explains to Beatrice that her daughter merely pitied a defenseless pawn of the matrimonial game. He also succeeds in convincing his niece that her bravado was sheer madness and urgent amends must be made. The next day, thanks to his diplomacy, Albert apologizes, even kisses the tutor, then proposes in a hurry. After Ági's manly exit, family honor is restored, the royal match is settled and the deposed house stands reinstated.

The title, the play's theme, is explained in the closing speech of Albert's haughty mother, Princess Dominica, who warns Alexandra to keep in mind the dignity of her position:

Remember that your saintly father used to call you his swan. Think often what it means to be a swan, gliding proudly, majestically, as the moon gleams on the mirror of the water, gliding away in the purple radiance and never coming ashore. For when a swan walks, my daughter, when she waddles up the bank, then she painfully resembles another bird! (427)

When critics called the play "a merciless satire of royalty," Molnár retorted: "It is simply a satire on meddling mothers, be they royal or otherwise."[26] Although Molnár does not hide his admiration for monarchy, the play is studded with satirical thrusts at the foibles of princely households. The general tone, too, is playfully ironic and mocking, especially at recounting the intrigues and machinations surrounding the prince's search for a suitable bride. Equally sardonic is the presentation of Albert's smug superiority, pompous mannerism, and ponderous phraseology. Beatrice's arrogant selfishness and superficiality in dealing with issues and underlings further substantiate the author's critical intent. In fact, Molnár quite openly criticizes royal disregard for the sacredness of the individual regardless of social origin. After all, Alexandra is compelled to forsake genuine love for family interest, and Ági is used cold-bloodedly as bait to catch a bridegroom. With unique skill, the author manages to present several unfavorable features of the royalty and still create a fair, even favorable picture. At the end the two dowagers' manipulations appear nothing more than ordinary commonsense concern for the children's happiness.

There is little novelty in the theme of a princess falling in love with a man of the people, but Molnár was not so romantic as to show a royal offspring sacrificing her future or a commoner running a dire risk to make her his own. Instead, he laughs and so do we, at the royal mother's pains to effect a proper marriage for a dutiful daughter.

Though the setting is a fictitious kingdom, it obviously takes place in Hungary, and Ági, the passionate idealist, full of rebellions and disdain for the ruling class, is definitely of Hungarian temperament; in fact, he passingly mentions that he was born in Transylvania. His compassionate portrayal is Molnár's proud tribute to his people. In contrast to the enervated and often silly prince, Ági is presented as a brave, masculine, brilliant man of integrity. Eventually, he earns even Albert's respect, who does not hesitate to state it: "Xara, he is a free spirit. He is not like us. With complete modesty he sat down at the table, and then with crescendo he lifted us to the skies . . . he remained up there but me he dropped to the ground. How elegantly he soared . . . ever upward" (425).

Characterization is remarkably subtle and effective; with diverting humor Molnár makes the whole cast identifiably human. It is not surprising that Ági's clever talk of the stars, the mischievous wisdom of Hyacinth, the matrimonial anxiety of the frustrated mothers, the punctilious concern of the majordomo, the meddling fuss of sister Symphorosa, and the bewildered contrition of Albert, leave an indelible impression on the audience. Each character is fully developed, vibrantly alive and credible, expressing emotional position with each word, with each gesture. Most unforgettable is the lovely Alexandra, obedient but thoroughly compassionate: she forgets her bargain with her mother, breaks down and confesses everything when she sees the suffering in the eyes of her guinea pig. She truly loves her poetic astronomer-tutor. The scene where she kisses him and seemingly destroys her own future is a perfect dramatic bravura deservedly dominated by the heroine.

The action, spectacularly set in high-class splendor, is swift and absorbing. The dialogues are graceful, rapidly moving, with admirable economy of words. There is a pleasing mixture of the romantic and the satiric, touching pathos and sophisticated raillery. The tone is gently mocking, tender and piquant, blending a more than usual amount of Molnáresque wisdom and suave wit. The English translation is accurate, though, according to Professor Gergely, "In its entirety, the American play emerges lighter in tone, perhaps less reverently romantic, inclined in spots toward farce. . . . That is, of course, what the play needed to make it palatable to Americans, for whom kings, princes, countesses, and all the royal paraphernalia exist as objects of romance and ridicule."[27]

The dramatic structure is faultless, designed with meticulously proportioned rise and fall of action. In the first act the royal background is eloquently laid and exposition is easily achieved by means of the bantering gossip of Alexandra's young brothers. Romance has full sway in the entire second act in which Ági's wooing temporarily overcomes the princess's upbringing and composure. After the dinner scene, particularly clever in its byplay of double entendre, the denouement comes inevitably. But it required real dramatic art to continue into the last act without a sense of anticlimax. The elements that contributed to a satisfactory end are Ági's dignified departure and the justification of the aristocratic tradition of royalty.

The Swan is still widely played, and its three American motion-picture versions also attract impressive audiences. It is rather interesting to note that this was Molnár's only truly successful play in England, and in France it earned him the cross of the Legion of Honor.

Inspired by *The Swan's* success, Molnár quickly revised and finished three one-act plays which opened as a triple bill called *Szinház* (Theatre), at the Hungarian Theater in 1921. Each play, *Az Ibolya* (The Violet), *Marsall* (Marshal), and *Előjáték*

Lear Királyhoz (A Prologue to *"King Lear"*) presented a slice
of life among the thespians, portraying them with similar irony
and sarcasm. However, in plot, theme, and level of artistry they
vary considerably, warranting separate treatment.

The weakest of the three, *The Violet*, a rewritten comic sketch
about actresses trying to obtain roles at any price, was surpris-
ingly the only one staged—although unsuccessfully—on Broadway during the 1930 season.[28] The plot features a gruff, middle-
aged producer-manager in the process of hiring chorus girls
for his new operetta. Provocatively, without inhibition, the candidates offer themselves to him to get a part. Repulsed by their
phoney amorous advances, he disguises himself as a clerk,
pretending to assist his composer, who takes his place as the
boss. When it turns out that one of the applicants is attracted
to him for himself, and expects no favor in return, the apathetic producer takes a fresh interest in life while the girl wins
a contract for her "violet-like" modesty.

"It's a jungle out there!" states Molnár, as he satirizes the
cynical practices of theatrical agents who consider actresses
as their harem. The author repudiates not only the loose morals
of budding stars but also those managers who emulate "the
sharks of Hollywood's fleshmarket." The play lacks originality,
complication, and, most of all, a decent plot. The situation is
artificial, the climax, highly exaggerated, the characterization,
unconvincing. The occasional witty twists and funny quirks
prove insufficient to save this trifling sketch.

Marshal, a sparkling variation on *The Guardsman*'s theme,
on the other hand, is a minor masterpiece and genuine "theater."
In the United States this playlet was performed briefly only in
small repertory theaters, although in time its revised version
served as movie and television scripts.[29] The plot is based on a
true story related to Molnár by his friend Zoltán Thomka, a Hungarian hussar. In the dramatization the author turned the soldier into an actor and the husband a baron, but otherwise left
the tale unchanged.

The drama centers around a young actor, an aging baron and
his ageless baroness whom they both love. The husband has a
tragic obsession: "There is no deadlier love than mine, he who
is in love at sixty is bound to die with it; I must be merciless

for my time is short" (457). The actor has an equally sincere, deep, burning passion. The woman, caught between two all-consuming emotions, is undecided and plays with both men. The actor arrives early at a hunting party and heedlessly confesses his feelings, urging the baroness to flee with him. The husband overhears the scene and while his rival is changing for dinner, tells his wife that he would never give her up. Later, when the host boasts with his "perfectly safe" English rifle, "Marshal," it fires "accidentally," while aimed at the actor, who jokingly denies that the bullet touched him. Soon, howevert, he turns pale and collapses. The wife faints and the baron begs the guest's pardon with masterly dissimulation. A doctor is summoned and during the wait a macabre tragicomedy enfolds. Though the baron stands revealed as a murderer, his wife sides with him in denying any foul play. In the ensuing scene—an unexpected dramatic somersault—the actor performs his greatest role: in a tension-filled monologue he announces that he only pretended to be shot to test his hostess. "I was only curious about my funeral. That's exactly what I've witnessed, I died as a forsaken dog. I've learned my lesson" (469). Thereupon he says farewell and drives away with the doctor, straight to the hospital, seriously wounded. Betrayed in love, with his illusion shattered, the doubly wounded man is forced to use the only weapon he owns—his art and skill as an actor—to escape the further humiliation of becoming ridiculous.

This effective minidrama comprises Molnár's central themes, stars his favorite character types, and employs most of his stage tricks. Precisely structured, the fast moving action is controlled with unerring technique. With subtle irony gleaming through every line of the vibrant dialogues, the tragic and comic elements are kept in proper balance. *Marshal* validates Molnár's reputation as a craftsman of language, plot development, and technique; it may also serve as an edifying lesson in playwriting.

A Prologue to "King Lear," an absorbing comedy about a cuckolded husband and theater people, was never produced in English but became a standard in most European repertories. The theme was again the juxtaposition of reality and illusion, but with a unique treatment.

The action begins in a theater shortly before curtain time of

a performance of *King Lear*. Preparations are interrupted when
the star, Bánáti, who plays Lear, arrives in panic because he
learned that his lover's husband, Dr. Ernő, and a friend, Dr.
Kiss, are chasing him. All the cast, the stagehands, and even
the fireman rush forth and form a cordon to protect him
when the two men storm in. The husband is a bespectacled,
pedantic professor of literature; his friend, a colleague at the
university. Ironically, Dr. Kiss is also after Mrs. Ernő, and the
husband was about to have it out with him when he discovered
the more immediate threat. So he allied with his potential rival
against the common enemy. By the time they come on stage,
Bánáti is already in his impressive Lear costume. The majestic
attire and the implicit evocation of the spirit of Shakespeare
arrest the husband; he is incapable of venting his anger upon
"the King." Bánáti, once his beard and crown are on, tran-
scends his mundane personality and acts with royal dignity.
During the conversation, he can only perform: having no language of his own, he quotes from the play, articulating ponderous lines, shedding Lear's tears. Facing such a hero, Dr.
Ernő cannot disabuse himself of his awe; he tries to whip up
his anger, but fails: "I'm a civilized being. . . . My wife's seducer
hides from me behind the mask and stands in the guise of a
majestic figure, an unhappy mythical king and father whose
fate has often stirred me . . . I'm paralyzed . . ." (438). When
the "Duke of Burgundy" remarks that "Shakespeare was a
drunken actor and his plays were written by Bacon," the professor launches a scholarly denunciation of the Baconian theory
and explains his views on drama. In the end, his energy spent
with the lecture, he gives up and departs, leaving the impression that he came only to look for reasons to forgive his wife.
Domestic peace is restored, although Dr. Ernő refuses to attend the evening's performance of his favorite tragedy.

This sardonic, Pirandello-like play is a merciless parody of
a deceived husband and sly actors. Molnár adorns the Shakespearean characters with so much authority that the play's actual
characters are compelled to admit their own lack of substance
and, after being deflated, they scramble off into their dim, makeshift reality. The pathetic husband evoking pity may emerge
almost as a classic tragic hero, but his encounter with the thes-

pians reduces the tragic impact. In fact, when the fuming scholars face the majestic "Lear," the play turns into a congenial *tour de force*. The shift in their attitude saves the play from becoming a melodrama. In the ensuing dialogues the style is highly eloquent and witty, studded with academic jargon and stage lingo. The Shakespearean quotations, criticism of literary critics, and other learned quips are neither obtrusive nor do they slow down the rapid pace of the action. The ingenious plot is orchestrated with faultless technique but structurally the play is too long for one act. Some of the monologues could have been pruned. These factors alone could have prevented its English staging.

VII   *Expressionistic Experimentations*

In the first part of the 1920s Molnár seemed to have run out of his familiar topics so his fancy turned to experimentation with different trends. In trying to demonstrate his versatility, the eclectic author was drawn to opposite poles of literary styles, Naturalism and Symbolism, as well as Expressionism and Neo-Romanticism. The results were a series of disappointing plays: *Égi és földi szerelem* (Heavenly and Earthly Love, or *Launzi*), *A vörös malom* (The Red Mill), *Az üvegcipő* (The Glass Slipper), and *Riviera*. He wrote these plays for Budapest's new star, Lili Darvas, the future Mrs. Molnár number three.

Heavenly and Earthly Love, a symbolic melodrama about insanity, was a dramatization of his novel *The Derelict Boat*.[30] The play opened at the Hungarian Theater in 1922, and a year later its American adaptation by Edna St. Vincent Millay, called *Launzi*, opened at the Plymouth Theatre on Broadway. Both productions drew mostly unfavorable reviews.[31]

The seventeen-year-old idealistic Launzi lives with her divorced mother, Claire, and the latter's lover Frederic, a wealthy, physical type of man. In defiance to the immoral ménage, the saintly daughter worships Imre, a sensitive, virtuous youth, who, quite suddenly, becomes infatuated with Claire. Her passion blighted, Launzi attempts suicide but is rescued and then taken to her father's home. The episode unhinges her mind. She escapes into death, pretending to be a corpse. Previously, in her farewell letter, she summoned Imre to stand by her coffin, hoping that "she can resurrect by hearing him declare his heavenly love for her." Determined to keep her tryst, she arranges her own funeral. With the connivance of her reluctant father—she threatens another suicide if her wish is refused—a bier of white satin is prepared, flanked by candles, mounted on a lofty dais of sable. There stands the stunned young man staring at Launzi's "corpse." But she is betrayed by her own weeping, and when Imre confesses that he still loves her mother, the girl passes beyond all borders of sanity. She sinks deeper and deeper into the hallucination that she is an angel in heaven. Four months later, when Christmas carolers, dressed like angels, visit the house, she steps out of the tower window, wearing paper wings, in an attempt to follow them. Shouting, "Children! Wait for me! I'm coming . . . to guard you and show you the way" (550), she jumps and dies. At last she can join her people, the pure, the innocent, the heavenly tenants.

The original title, suggested by one of Titian's canvases, at once connotes the primal conflict between divinely inspired, metaphysical love and carnal passion; celestial devotion and earthly desire. The virgin heroine represents unselfish, sacrificial love, while her mother is the epitome of the sensuous temptress, the eternal Eve. Launzi's tragic downfall is caused by her inability to endure multiple disillusionments. Her faith in the power of spiritual love is first broken by her mother's preference for Frederic to her father, an idealistic artist, then by her romantic idol's succumbing to lust. Paradoxically, Imre, who starts out as a hero, as Launzi's alter-ego, turns into an antagonist, partly responsible for her tragedy. In her total dismay—even her suicide is thwarted—Launzi finds temporary comfort in a pretense as a living death, a delusion that becomes increasingly real to her as time passes.

Since Molnár's characterization is inextricably tied in with the theme, the members of the cast around the heroine come across as functional, pragmatic types. Claire is a typical Molnáresque female: selfish, crafty, adulterous, materialistic and cruel, bored with her honest husband but enraptured by her lover's fierce, primitive passion. Frederic, equally sordid, is shrewd, immoral, and sophisticated—a natural man and a winner. Ivan, Launzi's father is the loser: poor, weak, and gullible, a caricature of deceived husbands. Imre in his dual role ultimately amounts to no more than a naive, slightly degenerate visionary poet who is swept away by an all-consuming physical desire. In the midst of these people Launzi merely subsists; she is a saint, a doomed, ethereal being, too pure and innocent to survive in such a sinful world.

Launzi's febrile nature strongly resembles Hauptmann's Hannele, but she also calls to mind such kindred figures of literature as Shakespeare's Ophelia, Goethe's Ottilie and Ibsen's Hedwig. In writing this play, Molnár must have been inspired by both Maeterlinck's mystical symbolism in *The Blue Bird* and Hauptmann's poetic fantasy in *The Sunken Bell*, a tragic tale of a fragile, sensitive artist who is destroyed by the brutal forces of common reality.

The play is heavily symbolical. Characters, setting, and props all serve as symbols; even Launzi's final death on wings is presented as a symbolic escape of a personified perfect goodness from the evil, imperfect world. The excessive use of celestial music, Christmas and funeral paraphernalia, the overabundance of white and gold colors make the already harrowing drama suffocating and scarcely bearable. The English version is set at a resort by the Adriatic Sea, where the "blue foamy waves" provide yet another symbolic overtone. These dramatic devices, however effective individually, appear overused here and weaken the play's impact. In *Launzi* the author tries to pitch on the altitude of a classical drama, but the rarefied literary air cannot sustain as much dramatic life here as did the light atmosphere of his social comedies.

Molnár's debased intent is all the more saddening because in this play his habitual cynical tone and satiric verve are replaced by sincerely felt pathos and consistently serious veracity. Indeed, this is the playwright's first genuine tragedy in which he aspired to employ all those "safe" techniques which never failed to move theatergoers. Admittedly, in parts the language reaches imaginative and genuinely poetic heights, particularly in the heroine's last stages of insanity, but by that time the already shocked and exhausted audience is unable to feel moved by the aesthetic beauty of some parts.

On the play's religious implications, the public reaction revealed a strange ambivalence. Death equally fascinates and repulses people, but few enjoy mock funerals, pseudo priests and nuns. Even fewer can revel in long, lunatic harangues like Launzi's address to her "sweet Jesus and Heavenly Advocate." She says, "I go to complain to Thee, who sorrowed in Gethsemane...O Man of Galilee! I go to complain to Thee, but to Thee I shall tell everything" (537). One critic dismissed the play as "too reverential," while others regarded it as "deliberately morbid, sacrilegious, bordering on blasphemy."[32]

The public depreciated Launzi's prolonged madness and scoffed at the grotesque framework in which someone becomes a living corpse on account of unrequited love. Such gross oversimplification can easily be disregarded, but even Molnár's most ardent disciples seemed disappointed with this drama. His friend Aurél Kárpáti praised the theme, which proved "that in our wicked capitalist society the pure has no place," but added that "this is a mini-*Faust* without Goethe...and one cannot fly with glued paper wings."[33]

Launzi was an overambitious work. The dramatist simply ignored his limitations and attempted to compress into one play too many varying techniques along with supernatural, unnatural, and pathological elements. Not even a well-constructed five-act play—as this was—can carry such a heavy load. Despite Molnár's popularity and Miss Millay's reputation, the play failed in New York as it did in Berlin and Vienna, where, by that time, the author was regarded as an "indigenous" playwright.

Undeterred by poor receptions, Molnár grew even bolder in his experimenting. His next play, *A vörös malom* (The Red Mill), a philosophical extravaganza, opened at the Hungarian Theater in 1923 under the able direction of László Beöthy, featuring Lili Darvas. Although grandiose in its scope, the play was another disappointment and, for the first time, the performance was met with open hostility. In fact, the Budapest premiere created such a violent controversy that the author was compelled to issue a statement defending his work. In New York it fared somewhat better. Adapted and directed by David Belasco, who called the play *Mima*, the glittering production opened in 1928 and ran 180 times.

This expressionistic, pseudoscientific satiric fantasy, was based on his short story "The Secret of the Aruwimi Forest," set in Hell, and was conceived as a comic morality play. In Molnár's words, it was "a theatrical jest which now and then grows deadly serious and will perhaps induce a tear or two."[34] Its slender plot is built around the notion that man is corruptible, but ultimately good conquers evil. The Magister, the Head Devil in Hades, has just completed the Red Mill, the "Corruptor Infernalis," which can transform even the best man into a beast within minutes. This fantastic contraption, like a witch's cauldron, contains: "iron, nickel, sulphuric acid, roses, curses, silk, opium, hate, love, pianos, mud, fern, bromide, clamshells, passion, vitriol, lentils, sweat of workers, laughters, sobs, and thyroid glands . . ." (557), just to mention a few of the ingredients. To test the machine before his majesty, the King of Hell and his court, the devils, at last find a truly virtuous man on earth, János, the gentle forester. They kidnap the meek fellow and toss him at once between the millstones. There he is ground up like wheat grains in a regular mill, like life grinds humanity. Under the Corruptor's soul-destroying pressure, his resistance is quickly broken and his virtues eroded. Soon he cheats, steals, lies, commits adultery, embezzles, deserts his pregnant wife, gambles, marries for money, and tortures his new spouse. The Stygian crowd is jubilant. But when János is about to kill his lover Mima, his last spark of virtue flares up and makes him forgive the now repentant siren. His change of heart confuses the Magister and the Corruptor blows up. Released from its power, János returns to his loving wife, Ilonka, waking up as though from a dream, to the smell of baked kraut, his favorite dish.

While putting good and evil on their inevitable collision course, the play promotes the moral according to which man is feeble, an easy victim of woman's lure, but his seminal divine spark cannot be totally extinguished. Every human mood and mode of behavior enters into the dramatic action and all sinful elements of our civilization are held up to criticism. Hypocrisy in particular is under heavy attack. Those who cover up their evil nature are rejected even by the devils; the Magister refuses to accept a self-righteous school principal, a soulful poet, and a civil servant—beware of them! Women are also reproached through Mima, the ultimate evil. As the reigning temptress of Hades, she symbolizes Everywoman and plays a major role in János's corruption. The antifeminist allusions coming from a notoriously debonair playwright sound insincere and incongruous. Men would not be overjoyed if the world were populated only by humble, sentimental females like Ilonka. Conversely, the bucolic happiness of the forester couple appears poignant, but boring, while the hero's erotic adventures with the wicked Mima have remarkable vividness and appeal.

The structure is complicated: the original play consists of a prologue, lasting for half an hour, and two parts in twenty-six scenes strung together in mutual action. The Belasco version has three parts in forty scenes. The setting includes an orchestra pit from which Satan and his court watch the performance. In the first two parts, the action of Hell's inhabitants—the framework of the play—takes place on the front of the stage before a black curtain which parts for each scene revealing various earthly happenings. In the third part the background is a red curtain behind which the Infernal "Computer" is constructed, perpetually moving, smoking, and emitting odd noises. Sixteen scenes are performed within the Red Mill's intricate steel portals. Further confusion is added by the malevolent disquisition of the Magister and his devils, who constantly interrupt the action. As the earthly dramas unfold, they go on clowning, making sly remarks from a platform. With these suave "asides" pronounced while carrying out various chores, they keep alive the illusion created by the machine's puppetry on the main stage.

This horrendous scarlet Inferno is crowded by numerous fiends, mannequins, and forty-one main characters: ten humans, fifteen devils, and sixteen puppets. The puppets used to be people on earth. After their capture, they were transformed into humanized mechanical creatures—controlled by the Magister—to personify certain human traits. Their leader is Mima who, when the machine disintegrates, metamorphoses into her former self. The horned devils, hooved, grotesque, and demoniacal, provide the comic relief. Their names Rubicante, Libicocco, Malacoda, etc., are borrowed from Dante's *Inferno*. The characters shift with no regard for time, space, or logic, apparently to keep the relationship between Hell and Earth in "harmony." In the Plutonic workshop of the third part, the action of the short, disconnected scenes moves in fast sequence like episodes in a modern science-fiction movie. The language is highly imaginative; a strange mixture of songs, aphorisms, legends, and ordinary dialogues, sometimes poetic, sometimes mundane and colloquial, sometimes profoundly philosophical. The devils' chanting and chaffing sound particularly humorous spiced with facile irony. Unfortunately, in the midst of the mass confusion, endless clamor and movement, the delicate thread of fancy is constantly disrupted, thus the style remains the least important dramatic device.

The play is a mastery of stagecraft; the Corruptor is manipulated by a special switchboard and moves on revolving wheels and snapping electric arcs. Numerous innovative techniques as well as complicated sound and light effects are employed: nonstop steam, fire, and smoke belching from the Mill, rumbling noises, organ music blending with jazz, shrieks of dancing demons, relentless flashes of red lights that accompany the acting. Even the audience is involved as extras, constituting the devil's court. In Hungary, Molnár himself helped to build and supervise the construction of the stage and the elaborate set. In New York, the production required a veritable rebuilding of the whole theater and the use of the adjacent auditorium as well as the stage.

Critics in Budapest regarded the play immoral, absurd, and distasteful. Why such a vast expenditure, they asked, to present a trite and banal sermon of the persistence of virtue in its contest with sin? In New York, the production appealed to those in particular who liked lavish spectaculars, but, in the opinion of Frank Chandler, "Molnár is on much safer ground when out of the infernal regions, dealing with the rule of polished folks of Budapest."[35]

Mima is little more than a grand-scale theatrical extravaganza, cleverly designed, ingeniously constructed, a fanciful experimentation with impressionistic techniques. Its ethical views and moral message are indeed superficial, rendered with ostentatious cynicism, aiming rather at jest than profundity and giving the impression that Molnár himself did not believe in his own sermon.

Having experimented with the supernatural realms, from heaven and hell Molnár now turned to earth and chose a low-class environment as the locale for his new play. *Az üvegcipő* (The Glass Slipper), as suggested by the title is a Cinderella story, and sounds innocent enough; yet, its premiere at the Comedy Theater in 1924 evoked violent reactions again and further alienated the once-pampered playwright from his native city. The play also aggravated his marital problems with his second wife, stirred up malicious gossip, and subsequently led to his divorce from Sári Fedák in 1925.[36] The disillusioned, bitter Molnár then moved to Vienna and started his long peregrinations in Europe.

The play failed in New York, too. After sixty-five performances and unusually vitriolic reviews, it closed in 1926.[37] The unfavorable reception seems somewhat unfair since the drama has considerable merits. But in Hungary during those years Molnár was engulfed by intrigues, slanders, and such destructive hostility that he could write nothing that critics would have found praiseworthy, whereas in the American performance the play's squalor overshadowed its inherent poetic pathos and social criticism.

Combining romance and realism, *The Glass Slipper* is a study of low life in a sordid boarding house, brightened by the character of its heroine, Irma, a sensitive, sentimental, nineteen-year-old servant, engrossed with romantic notions. Endowed with Barriesque imagination, she adulates the star boarder, Sipos, an aging carpenter whose room she has been cleaning for years. When he marries the landlady, Adele, Irma falls into despair. At the wedding, she reveals the bride's illicit affair with a young tenant. When Sipos fails to renounce his new wife, the lovelorn girl runs away, ready to throw herself into prostitution. As she is bargaining with the madam, the house of ill repute is raided by police, and Irma and all in the establishment are arrested. Next day, at the police court Sipos realizes the intensity of Irma's love and decides to get a divorce and marry his loyal servant.

The story is vulgar and implausible, lapsing into occasional sentimentality, but its characterization and satiric social criticism redeem it. The proletarian Cinderella is portrayed as an innocent child of nature, a frail, whimsical, pitiful drudge. In the coarse environment, her imagination is regarded as idiocy and soon she herself feels inferior to everyone. Yet, Irma maintains faith in the world of fairy tales. With pathetic devotion she endures her idol's abuses and seems transfixed with ecstasy each time "Prince Charming" appears. She cleans his room in a state of intoxication, kisses his pillows, talks to his clothes: "Oh, there is no more beautiful ray of life than he is, my only love and chain of roses, my violet forever" (630). Hers is the divine madness of the fairy story, enduring in filth, squalor, and brutalization. In the end her pure adoration conquers all, and her coveted "prince" finally "finds the lost glass slipper."

In contrast to Irma's painful impracticality and idealism, her "fairy stepmother," Adele, is a hypocritical, wicked shrew who secretly yearns to be decent. She marries Sipos to attain respectability, and she knows well that the young boarder professes love for her only to escape paying his rent. Adele's character is drawn with teasing cynicism and so is the carpenter's. The gruff, petulant, pompous Sipos, the iron-gray Don Juan, appears as a caricature of a voluptuary with a golden heart whose cruelty is mere facade. He exploits and ridicules Irma, calls her a "slut," but at the end, magnanimously accepts her "services."

The play reveals a delicate balance of class distinction among low class people. In this rigid hierarchy, Sipos and Adele are on the top by almost reaching middle class standards, whereas Irma stands on the lowest rung of the ladder. In between, each servant recognizes his own degree of rank: the chambermaid is higher than the menial help, the cook has privileges but not as much as a houseman. At the wedding, Adele's guests are "bona fide gentlemen, real classy people": an alcoholic ship-captain, a photographer, and an engraver. The most despised creatures, of course, are the prostitutes; the whole boarding house clan looks down on them with contempt. With fine differentiation, Molnár satirizes "respectability" at different levels of the social structure.

The Glass Slipper is well constructed: the first act is a brilliant exposition of the boarding-house ménage, a vivid panorama of genuine low-class characters realistically portrayed. The second is a kaleidoscopic wedding party where amid eating, drinking, and dancing to gypsy music the comic climax is achieved with calculated effects and quickening tempo. The third act, at the police station, featuring the whole cast, serves as an anticlimax and an exercise in dramatic irony. Irma remains in the background while the madam delivers a platitudinous speech about her profession. The comic spirit undergoes permutation here, and reality takes over, breaks the spell, and rends the dream.

The play's major strength lies in the dialogue; Molnár makes use of folk humor, professional jargon, and determines the characters' class status through their speech habits. Irma sometimes talks in verse but her poetic images are full of malapropisms and wrong usage. Adele's language is vulgar; the madam's is replete with affectations and banal clichés.

Molnár's Hungarian Cinderella story sets out to dramatize the fairy tale in an especially squalid surrounding. It is rather difficult to see the heartbreaking beauty in Irma's love for the shrinking, tobacco-smelling "Prince," twenty-nine years her senior. In fact, to reward her vision with the decaying flesh of a mean old man is a base betrayal. It is even more so if we accept the notion that the Sipos-Adele-Irma triangle was patterned after the author's relationship wih Fedák and Darvas. Edmund Wilson called Molnár "impertinent" for comparing his association with the young actress to that of Irma's adulation for the carpenter.

The Hungarian critics and trade union leaders were outraged by Molnár's cynical treatment of Sipos, claiming that he ridiculed the working class and made a mockery of the world's most honest profession.[38] Apparently the author's satiric intent misfired again.

Riviera, Molnár's next theatrical experiment, was another strange, tragicomic Cinderella story. For the first time a Molnár premiere took place in a country not his own. It opened in Vienna's *Josefstadt Theater* on December 23, 1925,[39] and in Budapest, at the Renaissance Theater, on January 12, 1926. In both places, the reviews were mixed and the audience reaction was discordant.[40] *Riviera* has not been produced on the American stage, but its movie script was televised on "Studio One" in 1950, as *The Girl of My Dreams*. The English translation by Francis Faragoh is included in *APM*.

The plot centers around Mr. Misch, a thirty-five-year-old sales clerk and his lover, Louise, a charming young salesgirl. When the play opens, Mr. Casella, the owner, an American millionaire, is visiting his store and falls in love with Louise. He invites the poverty-stricken girl to join him next day on a trip to the Riviera. The jealous Misch has long hated his nefarious boss, who used to be his roommate when they were young. After all, his rival became rich while he failed to succeed; and now the rascal wants to steal even his girl. The desperate clerk and the bewildered Louise get drunk during the night as they are preparing the season's window display, an elegant Riviera scene. In the glass cage, wax figures of Ford, Rockefeller, Jeritza, and a Russian princess are being dressed in fashionable outfits. Casella's own wax replica is also part of the exhibit. About midnight, the highly inebriated Misch shoots his rival's mannequin, "robs" him, puts on his clothes, and begins dressing Louise in the most glamorous gown of the show. Right in the shop window, he takes her on an imaginary tour at the luxurious resort. A mad, macabre game ensues. They carouse with the wax figures and disrupt the whole display. Illusion and reality become completely interwoven in their intoxicated state. After the rapturous dream comes the bitter awakening. In the morning, Casella comes for Louise. He tries to promote Misch to director, who indignantly refuses such compensation, but the lucky Cinderella "bequests" her jilted lover to another adoring salesgirl.

The thematic elements, love triangle, jealousy, and the conflict between the rich and the poor are regular favorites of the playwright, but Molnár intends to present a more profound theme here; he calls the play a comedy though it exudes more acridity than mirth. The social message is inherent: the rich are the winners no matter how heroic, proud, and honest the poor try to be. In essence, the play is an attempt to demonstrate the ridiculousness and futility of any low-class revolt against the powerful capitalist system. Casella's impressive, lifelike facsimile is the satanic symbol of money; he sits high above all the other figures, like Zeus, manipulating and controlling people's lives. Thus, Misch's hopeless minirebellion is nothing more than a persiflage of those naive attempts that try to disrupt the status quo. Conversely, the hero's revolt here is only symbolical: he shoots the mannequin of his exploiter, but in reality he bows

to the might of money. Indeed, he lacks any "proletarian consciousness" and has no real desire to alter the social order, but
rather aims to advance within the system into its ruling class.
The tone is skeptical and pessimistic, sometimes lapsing
into sentimentality. When Misch "kills" the boss and dismantles
the exhibit under the incredulous gaze of two workmen and
Louise, he shouts:

What am I doing? I, Misch, am having a fling. I, the dog, have turned
into a human being. I, the coward, found courage. Don't gape! Drink!
In this world this is the only way I can still get money and a dress
suit. Now you'll come with me to the Riviera . . . there will be sun,
ocean, ecstasy, pleasure, concert, and mayonnaise. (702)

The intrinsic bitterness, however, is disguised by the incorporated marionette play, and at this point the play disintegrates.
Wax figures cannot act, and, as one critic remarked, "Among
them the living, too, become wax dolls eventually. A play featuring such characters can never be genuinely dramatic, only
picturesque if all goes well."[41] Costumes, masks, mannequins,
and perfervid dream scenes inspired by alcohol can be thoroughly functional dramatic devices. In fact, the author already
utilized them abundantly in *The Red Mill*; but here, the rather
sophomoric, lengthy game with the wax figures simply does not
work. It appears forced and grotesque and fails to blend with
the otherwise realistic plot.

This play temporarily marked the end of experimentation as
well as failures. The vain and sensitive author came to realize
that people had not been entertained by his new games. Deeply
concerned about his declining fame, Molnár came to the conclusion that drawing-room comedy was his safe genre. Thus, in
less than a year he managed to create another theatrical masterpiece that brought him top listing again.

VIII   *The Pinnacle*: The Play's The Thing

After his angry exit from Budapest in 1924, there was a brief
repose in Molnár's hectic life. He finished *Riviera*, and a few
one-act plays in Vienna. In June 1926 he married Lili Darvas
and it was during this period that an incident occurred which

inspired his next play, *Játék a kastélyban* (Play in the Castle, i.e., The Play's the Thing). Molnár explained how it happened:

My wife [Lili Darvas] and I were stopping at the Hotel Imperial in Vienna. She was then learning to speak German. All day long she had to recite classical German plays. One afternoon an intimate friend called on me, and as we were chatting amiably, he suddenly jumped up. He had heard Lili's voice in her room saying in fluent German, "I love you, I love you! I shall die of love for you!" No wonder he jumped. And I jumped. Both of us went to the door and, upon opening it, found Lili reciting declarations of love to her tutor, Dr. Hock, the German director. Utterly harmless, yet how disturbing it sounded! That's how I got the idea, but you can just as well say that I got it from "Hamlet."[42]

This play instructed his audience in how to get out of an embarrassing situation and offered a living manual for playwriting. For the second time now in his career, the play's world premiere was not in Hungary but in Italy and in the United States. The play had a prerun at the Great Neck Playhouse in Great Neck, N.Y., in October 1926, and on November 3, 1926, it opened at the Henry Miller Theatre in the brilliant adaptation of P. G. Wodehouse. The Budapest production of the original followed on November 27, 1926, at the Hungarian Theater. In both places the comedy was an enormous hit and ran for a long time.[43] Soon it mesmerized audiences all over the world.[44]

The play's merit lies in its superb craftsmanship and theme, not in its uncomplicated plot. A dreamy young composer, Adam, accompanied by his older collaborators, Turai and Mansky, arrive unheralded at a castle on the Riviera. One of the other guests there is the composer's fiancée, Ilona, a well-known prima donna. While in the room adjacent to hers, they overhear a passionate conversation between her and a previous lover, Almady, a leading actor. The heartbroken Adam threatens suicide. Seeking a solution, Turai decides to concoct a play that will incorporate the incriminating phrases as part of the dialogue. Then he forces the repentant actress and her panic-stricken partner to learn and rehearse their complicated lines during the day. At night, the makeshift farce, "a French comedy," is enacted, with

Turai as stage manager. Adam is relieved to discover that his beloved was merely rehearsing the night before. Reconciliation follows, and Turai puts another feather in his cap as savior of indiscreet ladies.

Slight as the story is, it is developed with masterful technique. Turai the dramatist is Molnár himself, who controls and enjoys the action as he leisurely spins out its gossamer thread. He finds wicked pleasure in disciplining both the flirtatious, cunning Ilona and the pompous Almady, who submits to every indignity to avoid being exposed in a scandal. The sweaty old lecher is forced to copy out the whole script within hours, memorize an infinite variety of unpronounceable French names, and play the role of a duped buffoon instead of a flamboyant hero. The text makes him caress a "soft, round, fragrant peach" rather than the lady's shoulder. His protestation during the furtive rehearsal and comments upon him by the spectators are as comic as the maneuvers of the characters at the presentation of the play-within-the-play of A *Midsummer Night's Dream*. The scene works enchantingly as a triple travesty: of pretentious actors, French farce, and "The Play's the Thing," itself.

But Molnár does more than use the plot to develop an idea in a novel fashion; going far beyond the theme, he takes the audience into his confidence and teaches them how to write a play through Turai's reflections. Acting as a master of ceremonies, a trickster, and an omnipotent director rolled into one, he periodically expounds his dramatic principles and expostulates the secrets of stagecraft, somewhat after the manner of Pirandello in his *Six Characters* . . . or of Echegaray in his *Great Galeoto*. As the play opens, Turai is musing upon the difficulty of presenting the *dramatis personae*:

Of all the brain-racking things in the world, beginning a play is the worst. That's where your technique comes in, my boy. Take this scene here, for instance. We three—curtain goes up on three ordinary men. . . . If this were a play, we would have to start jabbering about a lot of thoroughly uninteresting things until the audience gradually found out who we were. . . . Think how much simpler it would be if we would just introduce ourselves. Ladies and gentlemen, good evening. My name is Sandor Turai. I am a playwright. . . . I bow and step back, leaving the stage to you. (730)

Forthwith his partners do just that while Turai continues his supercilious lecture about his profession; "after all, one is either a playwright or one isn't" (751). In similar fashion, he "writes" the end of the second act. Magnanimously, during the rehearsal he allows his collaborators to take the play out of his hands and propose curtain-lines. When Mansky suggests a sentimental toast as ending, it is given, and the curtain starts to descend. At Turai's objection, it lifts. When Adam substitutes a melodramatic suicide, again the curtain dips. But the "director" prolongs the suspense, orders it up again, and himself finishes the scene in a sensible fashion, summarizing how dangerous the revelation of the truth would be. At this tense moment he shouts: "*Now* let's have the curtain!" (761). What a clever gimmick! This is a self-confident dramatist's manipulation of both the audience and actors, as well as an ingenious method of enhancing the play's action. The third act proceeds without further intervention of the "author," but before the resolution, he provides additional, perfectly timed tomfoolery thereby managing to bring out the last bit of humor in the situation. Thus Molnár proves that the play is no more than a game, a sophisticated but slight charade—as if to demonstrate, with his customary cynicism, that every problem can be solved provided one has humor, ingenuity, and gamesmanship.

The play, however, is not as glib as it seems. It presents more than wizardly stage tricks and unctuous instructions about the art of drama. In an entertaining fashion, a venerated theater expert himself criticizes the art of pretense and gives a self-persiflage. This play clearly evinces that in Molnár's mind the line between theater and life was beginning to disappear; what he experiences in real life reappears in theatrical scenes: truth as illusion, pretense as reality. As in *The Guardsman*, he careens on the double-edged razor, on the crumbling borderline of stage and reality, saying with Pirandello that what goes on beyond the walls of the theater is not life but histrionics, another play. While involving the audience in the mystery of creating a play, he reveals that the spurious action on the stage is at least as "real" as life. Thus, a playwright provides no less than a chunk of life, featuring not fictitious characters but "real" people. Therefore, all of us are actors and our lives are mere role-

playing; after all, "the play's the thing." Conversely, the creations of the mind partake of a more valid existence than palpable
physical objects.

This play is Molnár's most dazzling, most mercilessly cynical
farce in which he surpasses his masters, Scribe, Sardou, and, to
some extent, even Pirandello, although not in depth but in
techniques. The characterization is consummate; the theater
folks are aided by a comic social secretary and a funny old
butler, Dwornitschek, a worthy cousin of Shaw's William the
waiter, or the adapter's Jeeves. The dialogues are sparkling and
witty, adorned with subtle quips and blatant gags. Wodehouse's
English version is as humorous as the original.

After the play opened, Budapest once more embraced its
prodigal son; critics and the public were equally overwhelmed.
"Molnár has given us an expensive gift," wrote Schöpflin enthusiastically; "with his complex game of entertaining, Molnár is
now peerless in Hungarian dramatic literature."[45] In New York,
the reviews seemed similarly laudatory, describing the play as
"fascinating, urbane, and highly imaginative," adding that "Molnár's complete relaxation, his witty dialogue and sly innuendo
refresh and exhilarate, leaving a piquant aroma of their humor
and still lingering for a long time."[46] Though he wrote his true
masterpiece, *Liliom*, seventeen years earlier, with this play the
controversial playwright reached the zenith of his dramatic
career.

IX   *Facile Farces*: Olympia, One, Two, Three,
and The Good Fairy

Having reestablished himself among the vanguard of European dramatists, with the fruits of *The Play's the Thing* bounti-
fully reaped, Molnár was able to sustain his popularity in the
following three years. Living in temporary tranquillity in Vienna,
attending gala openings of his plays all over the Continent,
rewarded by royalty, entertained by heads of governments, he
was indeed the peer of playwrights. It was also in this period
that he visited the United States for the first time and received
a hero's welcome in New York in 1928. Surrounded by glory,
the inspired author brought forth one suave comedy each year:

Olympia, Egy-kettő-három (One, Two, Three), and *A jó tündér* (The Good Fairy), which further enhanced his fame.

In the imperial atmosphere of the Austrian capital, Molnár's fancy turned again to romance among the aristocracy. Reminiscent of *The Swan, Olympia* presents a love affair while assailing the cruelty of royal exclusiveness at the expense of the common man. The play opened at the Hungarian Theater, in March 1928, to a rapturous reception. The press was almost unanimously enthusiastic and the audience was ecstatic. *Olympia* has been one of Molnár's most frequently performed plays in Hungary,[47] but the New York production, seven months later, was a startling disappointment: it closed after thirty-nine performances and received poor, unsympathetic reviews. The failure might have been due to the difficulty on the part of the American public to comprehend the play's social message and the hero's motive in rejecting the love of the princess. These features were fully understood by the European audience, and apparently by Hollywood as well. The several movie versions of *Olympia* fared far better than its stage production.[48]

The setting is a fancy Austrian spa just before the war. Olympia, the snobbish, haughty daughter of Prince Plata-Ettingen and Princess Eugenia, is charmed by Captain Kovacs, the handsome Hungarian hussar who storms the lofty lady persistently. Though she has remained in secluded widowhood for eleven years, Olympia now allows herself to be at least "impressed." But when Kovacs speaks to her of honorable love, she dismisses him with disdain and rejects his marriage proposal with the taunt of his peasant origin. The proud captain plots revenge. He spreads the rumor that he is an international swindler in disguise. The Ettingens are shocked, fearing involvement in a scandal. So ready are they to clean their skirts that Olympia assents to meet the impostor's demand that she give herself to him for once as a price of his disappearance. With the air of a martyr to the cause of preserving the good name of the court, she follows Kovacs to his room. In the morning it becomes evident that the slander was pure invention and he is indeed a captain—in fact, an old friend of Prince Ettingen. Olympia gladly offers Kovacs reconciliation and humbly confesses her love for him. But she is swiftly rebuffed. A Hungarian hussar cannot forgive an affront to his pride even by a woman he loves. His reply is icy: "You insulted me and I avenged myself. I owed that vengeance to myself and to every peasant in this world" (823). Then he clicks his heels and leaves the motionless princess with the memory of the night.

Molnár sets up an easily recognizable background of the status-conscious aristocracy by using stereotyped characters, almost caricatures, who represent the chief elements of a jaded society and its long-established traditions. Prince Ettingen, a general unconditionally loyal to the Emperor, is so firmly placed in his position that he can afford to associate with commoners. But Eugenia and her daughter take their social superiority seriously and shun the "vulgar mob." The relatives, Countess Lina and her husband, with their gossipy tongues, symbolize public opinion that awaits eagerly a misstep by the court ladies.

The Ettingens resemble the royal family in *The Swan*. Olympia, like Alexandra, is a proud, loyal, pretty daughter, ready to sacrifice love for family honor; Eugenia is the counterpart of Beatrix and the duchess, the intriguing, regal mother. She is Molnár's often-cast master of ceremonies dictating rules, designing schemes, setting traps, and solving conflicts. It is she who compels the reluctant girl to yield to the captain's outrageous condition: "Go! I've heard enough from you. I'm in command now. I give the orders" (801). Ettingen, like Prince Albert, represents the Monarchy. In both plays the victim is an honest, passionate Hungarian who retaliates for having been used as a clown, rebelling against the smug hauteur and sophisticated viciousness of the Austrian royalty.

And herein lies the meaning of the play. Behind the captain's harsh exit line lurks the Hungarians' resentment of the Austrian Monarchy. Kovacs represents not only a social class but also an entire nation. His ruthless revenge on Olympia must be interpreted as the realization of his responsibility to restore the self-respect of his class. Moreover, he avenged the abuse of his people by the arrogant ruling class of another people, rather than the wound inflicted upon his personal pride.

Without this social clue the play appears—as it did in New York—a mere farce or satire on the hysterical effort of royalty to avoid calumny. The comedy indeed lends itself to various interpretations. It can be viewed as a "Prince and Pauper" story. Difference in social status between lovers often constitutes the *raison d'être* of dramatic conflicts. But here the crisis is tamed into a bittersweet comedy. As one critic explained: "Molnár satisfied the snobbery of the Budapest bourgeoisie: they enjoy watching aristocrats even on stage. By the same token, the play suited their deep-rooted democratic feelings: a commoner won and the ruling class was ridiculed."[49] Obviously, the American public could not understand the play in this spirit. For them to be called a "peasant" was not a fatal epithet but an anachronistic label for a farmer. To them *Olympia* was a "tenuous story full of platitude; a high comedy beaten thin" in which the climactic, crucial last sentence sounded "exasperating."[50] Even S. N. Behrman, a noted Molnár enthusiast, criticized *Olympia*, calling it "a much strained, mediocre work."[51] It was this lost social implication which reduced the play's significance. On the other hand the audience, both in the USA and in Europe, responded positively to *Olympia*'s other features, primarily to its human theme.

Incorporated is Molnár's variation on a sour Molière axiom, according to which not even the finest woman can be conquered by honest means or without a mask. Thus, the open-hearted lover loses, while the impostor wins. Furthermore, it proves that women are stimulated by danger and taking risks. *Olympia* is the tale of a woman playing with fire—one of the old mainstays of Molnár's work. The heroine gets scorched in the course of her fiery flirtation with the Hungarian hussar, but not enough to destroy her. In high society etiquette and propriety prevail over individuals.

In 1965, Lili Darvas returned to Hungary to perform the role of Eugenia in *Olympia*'s revival. While one Marxist critic described the play as "a cotton candy, big, fluffy and sweet, leaving a lasting taste on our lips,"[52] another hastened to add, "Our proletarian consciousness is gratified when the 'peasant' officer leaves the flabbergasted princess revenged."[53] Since then, *Olympia* has been running almost continuously in Hungary's theaters. Molnár's second royal romance triumphs in spite of its cynical social message.

One, Two, Three, the comedy of speed, is a one-act play in which cynicism gives way to benevolent satire as Molnár burlesques the rapid efficiency with which capitalists transacted business in the 1920s. The play was first presented in 1929, at the Comedy Theater, along with the revived *Marshal*. The production got favorable notices in Budapest, but in New York, double-billed with *Violet*, it folded after forty performances in 1930. *One, Two, Three* was published in a slightly revised form, entitled *President* in the author's 1952 American play collection.[54]

The minuscule plot is built around Norrison,[55] a banker and Napoleonic dictator of a colossal Central European financial concern, who is imbued with the true American spirit. He is about to leave for vacation when he learns that his house guest, the lovely Lydia, has committed the unspeakable blunder of secretly marrying Anton, a Socialist taxi driver. Since her rich American parents—his most important clients—are due to arrive momentarily, the mogul must perform a miracle. Since he fails to break up the union (the couple love each other and the bride is already pregnant), he can only work to elevate the bridegroom to a station that the American magnate will approve. But to do this, he must act as quickly as a magician who cries, "One, two, three!" and then performs his trick. With great show of speed and skill, the Norrison organization shaves, clothes, adopts, appoints, certifies, and assigns social standing: titles, position, party and club memberships, health certificate—and all are bought within minutes. In front of the audience the burly, uncouth cipher Anton Schuh is transformed into the sleek, supercilious Count Dubois-Schottenburg before the unwitting parents arrive. In addition, a splendid nuptial feast is arranged and a honeymoon is mapped out with hotel reservations confirmed. Anton also obtains a bank account and a car. All this happens in less than an hour. After his job is done, Norrison takes his planned vacation on schedule.

The play starts out as a farce, but as the tempo increases it turns into a burlesque; the action is exaggerated and the characters become caricatures. With pointed asides Norrison indomitably throws unctuous compliments where salve seems necessary. In his bland manner, he appears so infernally omnipotent that it passes beyond the bounds of seriousness. Lydia plainly caricatures the impressionable American girl whose puritanical upbringing cannot withstand the Continental freedom of morals. Anton is a spoof of the anticapitalist youth who takes advantage of the exploiters when an opportunity arises. The staff members, mobilized to metamorphose Anton, are used as vehicles to satirize legal trickery, commercialized titles, and efficient creation of impressive appearances which are achieved not seldom by opprobrious means.

As in his novel *The Hungry City*, Molnár again demonstrates that everything can be purchased with money, and that our society is dominated by false values and pretenses. If the author meant to criticize, however, he does so only in Norrison's exit line: "I can be proud and I am, too. But as regards to mankind . . . after what was just done here . . . I think, *almost* all mankind . . . should damn well be ashamed of itself" (77).

The language is witty and the pace is phenomenal, but the essential message is lost in the delivery. As one American critic pointed out: "Since no dramatic complication arises and no character develops, the play hammers at one idea until the life is beaten out of it."[56] *One, Two, Three* is more like a gleeful raillery, replete with bons mots, than "an acerbic repudiation of Capitalism" or a conscious social satire, as it is viewed now in Hungary.[57]

Plays travel in strange ways. Molnár's next fanciful comedy, *The Good Fairy*, had a reverse fate: it became amazingly popular in the United States and several European countries, but in Hungary, after opening at the Comedy Theater in 1930 with mixed reviews, the play perished and has not been revived. In New York it ran for two consecutive seasons despite the negative opinion of the critics,[58] and its movie versions also met very favorable receptions both in 1935 and in 1947. In 1951, the play was turned into a long-running musical comedy under the title of *Make a Wish*.[59]

This fairy tale for adults is built around the hilarious machinations of an impulsive do-gooder, Lu, whose naiveté is so vast that she turns the lives of four unrelated gentlemen upside down. Working as an unassuming movie usherette, she seems so alarmingly innocent and trusting that an eccentric waiter volunteers to protect her from the city fevers. Soon she attracts the slightly less paternal eyes of a paunchy, rich millionaire, Konrad. To escape his advances Lu tells him that she is married to a lawyer. When the adamant suitor offers to make her husband wealthy by tactfully appointing him as legal advisor to compensate for her love, our desperate good fairy picks a lawyer's name, Dr. Sporum, at random from the phonebook and gives it to Konrad. She thus sees a way of playing the good fairy by turning her patron's generosity into help for Sporum, who turns out to be an indigent, straightlaced, Bible-reading bachelor. His professional integrity prevents him from accepting shady cases, therefore he is almost bankrupt. But even the highly principled lawyer falls prey to her: unable to resist such a break, he reluctantly accepts the nefarious commission. She feels that, as her husband, Sporum will make it possible for her to promote a good cause even though she becomes a kept woman. At the last minute, however, the impulsive fairy changes her mind, spends the night with the waiter, and becomes engaged to him. The duped Konrad withdraws his contract, whereby both Sporum and his alleged wife remain uncontaminated by dishonest money. The curtain falls on Lu advising the confused lawyer about the advantages of other professions.

But the play does not end here: an improvised epilogue follows in which the manager of the theater steps forward begging the audience for patience. He announces that the author has shown what happens to the characters afterwards. The scene opens as the entire group gathers at the hotel where the first act unfolded to celebrate Lu's tenth wedding anniversary. She is married not to the waiter, who is still "protecting" young, gullible maids, but to Metz, a middle-aged ex-statesman whom Konrad made his executive secretary at Lu's request. Sporum has married his secretary and became a professor. All these men have prospered in some magical way through the instinctive, illogical, and often blundering manipulations of the good fairy.

Molnár's motive might have been satiric, but barring the occasional cynical thrust, the play is neither farcical nor convincingly fanciful. The author tries to show how a genuinely altruistic girl, completely devoid of any moral sense, can, with all her idiocy, still be led intuitively to happiness for herself and others. The illusory world where such miracles are possible is created by Molnár's characterization of Lu. She exudes an ethereal aura almost appearing as a mere symbol. She keeps referring to herself as a fairy: "Titania . . . that *should* have been my name . . . or Puck, perhaps. We possess the magic of life and bring good luck to people" (248). Accordingly, she acts petulantly and with unselfish abandon. "I only make mistakes when I think. . . . I have no logic, only instinct. But when I do something blindly I always hit the mark" (234), she boasts. In this implausible, lunatic role that combines self-worship and altruism, Lu manifests her sincere desire to make everyone happy in a rather odd fashion. The means by which she carries out her so-called "mission" seem ridiculous and tasteless: she allows each man to undress her by a rationale such as: "I have a nice little figure so I let the poor boys see it. It makes them happy" (248). Sporum correctly states, "You're not a fairy—you're a little goose" (246). Yet she continues to act aloof, almost transcendental. Still, she does not come across as a symbol of the archetypal girl-wife-mother-lover figure Molnár meant her to be.

In fact, Molnár's slim symbolism remains a mere cover-up for her unscrupulous frivolity. As a result, the seriously meant play turns into a convoluted, garish burlesque. Under the veneer of sophisticated fantasy, the playwright produced a jovially babbling, mediocre boulevard comedy. The characters are aggrandized unproportionately: Konrad is almost omnipotent and too flatulent; the waiter is overly flippant; Metz acts too obstreperously both as a drunk politician at first, and as a content husband in the end. Only Sporum's presentation is realistic. The honest but muddle-headed, aging lawyer, near destruction, emerges as a tragicomic figure and serves as a catalyst among his unconvincing partners.

Technically, *The Good Fairy* is a fairly well carpentered work of a conscientious craftsman who knows all the tricks of the trade. The dramatic devices, however, are used too deliberately and the scattered incidents are loosely tied together. After the sequential, realistic three acts, the pseudo-Pirandellian epilogue seems incongruous, leaving the impression that Molnár has grown bored with the play and could resolve the twisted plot only with a trivial stage gimmick.

This unconvincing farce entertains periodically, but the author's ravishing humor appears to be petering out. And so does his creative energy. *The Good Fairy* concludes the "Golden Era" of the playwright's dramatic career, foreshadowing his general decline in the next decade.

X Plays of the 1930s

In the 1930s Molnár grew grim: suffering from insomnia, overcome by anxieties, depressions, and nostalgia for his youth, the social lion became a recluse. The rise of Fascism and what it portended made the Jewish playwright agitated and restless. During this tumultuous decade both his artistic accomplishments and his popularity abated, even though he wrote assiduously, bringing out gradually deteriorating dramatic works every year till 1937. These plays were still performed with varying success in his native city, Berlin, Vienna, and Rome, but no longer on Broadway. For almost ten years his name in America appeared only in film reviews when movies based on his old and new plays came out. The comparatively feeble but still technically polished plays of this period seldom echoed Molnár's customary humor, acerbic wit, and dramatic excellence. By and large, they were formulaic, predictable pieces, dilutions of his former accomplishments on stage.

Arthur, or *Valaki* (Somebody), a drawing-room comedy bordering on absurdity, is plotted around a phantom husband contrived by a pair of cunning crooks. The play opened at the Belvárosi Szinház (Downtown Theater), in February 1932 and moderately entertained the Budapest audience for the rest of the season, but it was revived only in 1975. The American premiere in P. G. Wodehouse's brilliant adaptation—included in *RC*—took place on March 12, 1978, at a small off-Broadway theater.[60]

This comedy presents three typical Molnáresque characters in a rather atypical conflict. Edith, the mysterious *femme fatale,* a devious divorcée and ex-nightclub singer of dubious age, yearns to settle down and lead a normal, married life. Her intended Robert, a member of the British aristocracy, prefers to flirt with other people's wives rather than marrying them. Her father Cortin, an international swindler just released from jail, comes to the daughter's aid. Together they play a grand scheme: they invent Count Arthur Ghuye, the ideal husband. He is a rich explorer who never stays at home. Posing as her lawyer, Cortin buys a castle with the wealth Edith received from generous lovers. Now properly staged, the self-appointed countess begins to receive letters from her "husband." To make the fictive spouse's existence more credible, Cortin supplies baby pictures, mementos, golf clubs, clothes, and sends frequent telegrams, magazine articles, even donations to the Church, in Arthur's name. Soon, not only Robert but the whole community acknowledges Count Ghuye as her husband. He is so much alive that lenders appear to collect old debts and even a paternity suit is launched against him. Edith pretends to be heartbroken over Arthur's dishonesty and accepts Robert's tender comfort. It now seems that Arthur has accomplished his mission. A telegram duly brings the news of his "untimely" death in Africa. Robert consoles the bereaved widow and announces, "Your past is dead . . . your future belongs to me" (177).

Arthur is a weak expansion of the illusion versus reality theme in *The Play's the Thing*, and a variation on the message of *One, Two, Three*, that appearances make a man. Molnár spells it out through Cortin, who says, "Who wants a man in person these days? People only want his . . . his radiations. He pays taxes, so he exists. He has a bank account, so he exists. He writes letters to the editor, so he exists. Who cares about his hundred and sixty pounds of flesh and blood" (142). A la plastic surgery, Cortin performs plastic psychology. Amazingly enough, he succeeds.

Harmonia (Harmony), "A Family Idyl with Chorus," has never been translated into English. It was first performed on October 7, 1932, at the Hungarian Theater. The play's curious further reception was described by the author himself:

Harmony was a noisy flop in Vienna. So noisy that a correspondent titled [it] "Theater Brawl in Vienna."

Actually the play is a romantic family comedy. The Hungarian premiere at Budapest a few months before had enjoyed if not a great, at least a decent success. But apparently the play had in it something offensive to the German-speaking public, in which the National Socialist sentiments already predominated.

The male lead is the president of an amateur choral society. The

Austrian opening was shortly before Hitler seized power. By then all
German choral societies were National Socialists to the core.[61]

Molnár was not aware that the play might carry political ram-
ifications when he parodied a hypocritical, pious "song-monster,"
the hero of his comedy. Yet, the ruthless caricaturing of a familiar
figure hit a sensitive nerve and cut deeply into the recently
strengthened consciousness of the Nazis. Such reaction was indeed ironical because nothing was more alien to Molnár's nature
than to foment political emotions. His motive was simply to mock
a deceitful pillar of society, who used music to camouflage his
misdemeanors.

The scene is Budapest in 1910. Kornely, a high-ranking coun-
cillor and leader of the local choir, is about to celebrate the
twenty-fifth anniversary of his music career. On the surface, he
is an ideal man of impeccable moral fiber: doting husband,
loving father, patron of the poor, champion of virtues, respected
and worshiped by all. Just before the festive banquet starts, it
is revealed that he has a mistress. Ilona, his docile wife, is shocked
and slaps him in front of everyone. Immediately she regrets her
harshness, and to make amends she grants permission to the
lovers to continue their affair discreetly. The open scandal is
averted by music: before the jealous fiancé of Kornely's lover
can confront his rival, he continues conducting the choir. The
music-loving youth calms down and joins the singers. Harmony
rules again.

Underneath each comedy lurks a diluted tragedy. *Harmony's*
emotional scale is suspended between two extremes: hearty
laughter and swallowed tears, burlesque gaiety and biting irony,
humor and pathos. Only in an illusory world or fantasy can one
achieve total harmony of love, marriage, success, and happiness.
Shangri-la is a coveted dreamland of all people. Molnár focuses
on a family where everything seems all right, where everyone is
happy and content, where peace and serenity prevail. Suddenly
it becomes obvious that in reality nothing is right. Kornely is an
inveterate lecher who carries out his debauchery among the
chorus girls—the most recent of whom is his manicurist; his
daughter's marriage is in shambles; and not even his love of
music is purely altruistic or artistic. All this comes to light when

Kornely's face is cut by a lovelorn barber, the jilted fiancé of the manicurist. The jealous youth cuts not only into his rival's skin but also into the phoney frame of middle-class morality. In the midst of the jubilant chanting, Ilona's resounding slap smashes the glittering facade, and the petty bourgeois castle of cards collapses.

At this point the play could turn into tragedy: the wife's illusions are irrevocably shattered, the barber's hopes are crushed. The action is careening on a razor's edge. But Molnár comes up with a safe solution: he lets the plot lapse into unreality. As a supporting theme, the play aims to show the magic of music. As the song of Orpheus tames the wild beasts, so is equilibrium restored by the choir's singing Kornely's harmonized composition, accompanied, of course, on a harmonium.

> My heart, my heart, my poor heart, stop drumming,
> Throb gently, tranquilly,
> Even if you're filled with emotions,
> With wondrous, sweet love,
> Love.
> Starry sky,
> Only you know my sorrows,
> You, silent stars
> Don't ever betray me.
> Towards you throbs,
> In great secrecy,
> Gently, sweetly, tranquilly
> The heart,
> The heart,
> The heart.[62]

Thus, music becomes a dramatic persona. For the first time, the playwright, an accomplished musician himself, uses singing as a thematic and structural device. Each act is concluded by songs, and their texts are suited to sharpen the contrast between reality and pretense.

Corresponding to the ironic subtitle, the disharmonious *Harmony* holds a distorted mirror to middle-class morality, while strangely paying tribute to the power of art. Through music Molnár ridicules recognizable types by presenting a satire of bourgeois family idyl. Though the characters are credible and alive enough, the conflict is drawn out of proportion and lacks satisfactory resolution. On the whole, the play fails primarily because of its overt sentimentality.

Sentimentalism was again superabundant in his next drama, *Csoda a hegyek közt* (Miracle in the Mountain), completed in 1933. The play was published in Hungary the same year, but it had to wait for three years for performance. In 1936, the Comedy Theater chose to celebrate its fortieth anniversary with the presentation of this controversial Molnár piece. It was not published in English, but New York's Playhouse Theater brought it out on April 26, 1947, under the direction of the almost seventy-year-old author himself.[63] The play was a tragic flop: it folded after three performances.

This legend in four acts, portraying the imaginary return of Christ to prevent a terrible injustice, takes place in the last century in a remote Carpathian village. The four-year-old son of little Cili, a downtrodden, simple servant girl, disappears. When his blood-stained cap is found, the mother is falsely accused of murdering her illegitimate child, fathered by the powerful mayor of the village. She is jailed awaiting trial. The desperate girl has no chance of winning unless some miracle occurs. When the court gathers, a mysterious lawyer appears from nowhere and listens to the jury declare the death penalty for Cili. Then, amidst consternation, he begins to talk and proves not only that Cili is innocent but, describing the crime, reveals the real murderer: the mayor. When the mayor denies the charges, the strange advocate leads the court to a rosebush in the forest and unearths the boy's body. The accused man breaks down, confesses, and goes insane. As the crowd watches horror-stricken, the lawyer resurrects the child—after he had been buried for months—and gently leads him away to heaven as angels sing from above.

Molnár's theme is clear: truth triumphs even though it is on the side of the poor, but that is a miracle: God's work. The play juxtaposes the social conflict and the conflict between faith and reason. In the end, Christ pronounces the theme: "Do not try to find an explanation—all explanations are wrong. The only correct one is one that nobody is looking for."[64] Unfortunately, the message is not skillfully communicated. The tight traditional structure is unsuitable. The social message, that only God can help a poor creature like Cili, is also lost in the tear-soaked delivery. The play was fiercely criticized. Osvát described it as "a cheap, delirious ranting, studded with convoluted symbolism, a dastardly escape to Catholic mysticism: a pseudo-legend treated with the most conventional stage methods."[65] Babits decried it as a work in which "sentimentality stands stark naked; it is the very genre built exclusively on tear-jerking that the French call melodrama."[66] Only Kárpáti ventured some praise: "At first the play seems like an antithesis of *The Devil*: both the lawyer and Mr. Miller are ubiquitous and know everything. Yet, this work is more akin to *Liliom*, another hymn of forgiving love."[67] In New York one critic remarked, "It has all the falseness of the worst written novels of the last century, and seems boring and dated."[68]

This most uncharacteristic Molnár piece, his first religious play, was written during an extremely troubled period when the playwright was in a state of depression triggered by malicious intrigues at home and occasional negative criticism abroad. Feeling empty and alienated, he locked himself up in a tranquil hotel in Cannes, and without talking to anyone for months he became immersed in the study of the New Testament.[69] Temporary setback, of course, is no excuse for an inferior artistic creation. Perhaps it would have been more beneficial if the author also had stopped writing for a while.

But he did not; instead, he finished another play, *Az ismeretlen lány* (The Unknown Girl), sometimes referred to as *The Girl from Triest* or *The Harbor Girl*, which sounded somewhat less pessimistic but no more artistic. At best, it served as a mediocre movie script.[70] Following the Budapest premiere at the Comedy Theater in 1934 and its short run there, the play was forgotten. In fact, this was the first full-fledged Molnár piece that has not been produced even in German.

The three-act play, with a huge cast of twenty-eight, opens at a cheap bar in Triest. Annie, the shoddy entertainer, joins the tipsy Count Armalia, who saunters in one night after having won a fortune in the casino. Overcome by generosity, he offers the unfortunate adventuress four weeks' stay in an exclusive sanatorium to cure her alleged lung illness. The rest of the plot transpires in the luxuriant Tyrol resort, showing how Annie tries desperately to stop the clock. Cunningly disguising her identity, she adjusts easily, fancying herself a woman of mystery. When the witching hour strikes and the count's payments cease, she remains, hoping against hope that she can become a permanent member of fine society. To this end, she pretends to fall in love with a wealthy guest, Rudi, whom she tries to coax into making a marriage proposal. Meanwhile, she sleeps with the local postal clerk to pay for such invaluable services as stealing all incriminating letters and cutting the phone connection between the count and the sanatorium's manager, who begins to worry about her unpaid bills. When the postal clerk is caught, and the truth becomes known, Annie kills herself.

Like most Cinderellas who overstay their time, the girl with ambitious dreams must pay a price; but why so high? Molnár intended the play as a social criticism, showing how rigid class structure and prejudice destroy people's hope for advancement. Instead, he produced a sentimental melodrama lacking credibility, whose conflict was again contrived and unconvincing. The play is filled with *non sequitur* incidents and dialogue that convey nothing. The characters are stripped of every semblance of reality and the action is no more than a senseless parading of puppets. Annie's actions are motivated by nothing more than her desire to prolong the masquerade at any price. Regrettably, Molnár failed to execute the rich possibilities inherent in his theme.

In April 1935 two new one-act Molnár comedies opened in Budapest, at the Andrássy-Street Theater: *A cukrászné* (Delicate Story) and *Mennyegző* (The Wedding).[71] Both went virtually unnoticed. In 1940, the author rewrote and expanded the former into a three-act piece which was presented at the Henry Miller Theatre on December 4 the same year. New York took a special interest in the play. More than eight years had elapsed since Molnár's last new play appeared on Broadway and it was the refugee playwright's first opening in his adopted country. But the anticipated reward did not materialize. Receiving disappointing reviews, the show closed after a three-week run.

Three familiar Molnár characters appear in the play: a dull, jealous, middle-aged husband, Henry Cristof, owner of a delicatessen; his bored, romantic wife, Mary; and Odry, a handsome young Frenchman, a frequent customer. Ostensibly, Odry is chasing the flirtatious proprietress, but the young man's pretended attention is by no means amorously motivated. The penniless youth secretly woos his pretty fiancée, while he enjoys the free food and money provided by the unwitting, ardent woman. In her menopausal infatuation, Mary is determined to make her recalcitrant Adonis happy, and manages to arrange furtive dates with him. During one clandestine meeting, while they are traveling in a cab, the driver gets involved in an accident. When Mary is summoned by the police as a witness, the shocked husband finds out about the peccadilloes and confronts Odry. The cynical idler tells Henry how he was lured into the affair, concluding: "It's a delicate story! Had it been left to me she'd never have known but . . . actually, I'm happily married and ready to leave."[72] The disillusioned Circe guiltily returns to tend the store; Odry, now a proud soldier, goes to the front; and the marital crisis is over.

In the original Hungarian script, the meager plot and character development suffice for an unpretentious one-act comedy designed to entertain contemporary theatergoers. Set in Budapest in the early 1930s, the conflict reaches its climax when the illicit affair between a romantic, restless, middle-aged woman and an unscrupulous young man is discovered by her jealous husband, and the youth reveals that he got married in the meanwhile. The heroine's love here is only motivated by her yen for adventure and excitement—a familiar Molnár theme.

In the extended English version, the story is placed into Switzerland, and unfolds during the war. Mary's passion here is aroused by "patriotic duty" to make "a perhaps soon fallen, heroic soldier" happy for the last time. Unfortunately, the playwright did not have enough new material to satisfactorily fill a full-length play; as a result, the American three-act variation became a painfully overwritten piece in which Molnár's long missed wit and quizzical humor flash up only occasionally. As one review stated, "The action stretches out as far as a string of spaghetti would if used as a transatlantic cable; the play is dull and dire except for a short scene at the police station."[73]

This episode is genuinely blithe. When the distressed Henry

appears at the precinct to find out why Mary was summoned, he sends in his calling card bearing only his name. The captain begins to shout:

Henry Cristof—nothing else. No occupation, no address, nothing. How am I to know what kind of a man he is? A boot-black? A banker? He simply has his name printed. . . . As if everyone was expected to know . . . Henry Cristof. Like Henry Ford. This world is full of strange people![74]

As the poor man is simmering anxiously, wondering about his wife, the garrulous captain keeps rambling about his calling card. Finally, he learns the truth, and a lesson as well: "You are *not* Henry Ford. . . . You must resign yourself to that."[75]

In the final analysis, *Delicate Story* is neither delicate nor delicious despite its suggestive, punning title; it is merely a jejune tale, as fragile as the bourgeois morals it aims to satirize. Indeed, the play is like a piffling piece of pastry containing just enough sugar and flour to make a brittle one-act tea biscuit. Regretfully, its dough rises to a three-act, giant puff with a large vacuum inside, short of substance and taste.

In October 1935 there was another Molnár opening in Budapest, this time at the Comedy Theater. *Nagy szerelem* (Great Love) received the same luke-warm reviews as the previous play had. In America only a rather weak movie was released, based on the play's script, of which no adequate English translation has ever been made.[76]

The plot is simple. After their father's death, the Ági sisters become impoverished and work as dressmakers. Margit, the serious-minded, martyr type, acts as a mother substitute, sacrificing her life to care for her light-headed sister, Irén, who is irresponsible and fancies herself a potential actress. Margit hopes Irén will marry her fiancé, Lajos, their pedantic, solemn, dependable tenant. But Irén loves Iván, an elegant, older married man, a film director. When Margit discovers their furtive affair and meets the ingratiating intruder, she, too, is smitten by his charm and masculinity and, for the first time in her life, she falls in love. Soon Iván gets a divorce and, despite Margit's vehement objections, marries Irén and the newlyweds leave for Hollywood.

The betrayed sister confesses her passion to Her Ladyship, the girl's rich patron, bitterly remonstrating about Irén's stealing her only great love. The wise old patron cunningly brings Margit and Lajos together; shortly both seem willing to resign themselves to little love.

The trite, predictable plot, somewhat reminiscent of Molnár's earlier comedy, *Fashions for Men*, is handled with the author's customary technical skills. Excellent timing and snappy ripostes often brighten up the dialogue, providing light entertainment. But ultimately, none of the dramatic devices serves any purpose; it is an insipid story featuring banal nonentities. What a pity that Molnár repeatedly wasted his playwriting talent! In spite of his efforts to portray the social ambiance of the 1930s, *Great Love* delivers nothing more than a platitudinous, uninteresting story of two sisters' love duet.

The premiere of the next comedy, *Delila* (Delilah) was a tragic landmark in Molnár's life. This was the last performance he attended in his beloved Budapest during the final visit to his homeland, and marked the conclusion of his dramatic career in "old" Hungary. It was also his last truly humorous play, still reverberating his comic acumen, ineffable urbanity, and dazzling wit. On the opening night, September 17, 1937, at the Pesti Szinház, the enthusiastic audience cheered both the playwright and his wife, Lili Darvas, who played the leading role. After two weeks Molnár left Hungary, not knowing that he would never return. Ten years later, in New York, Sam Jaffe translated the revised script as *Blue Danube*, included in *RC*. The play never made it on any American stage, but it was filmed in Hollywood.[77]

The action takes place at a roadside restaurant, "Blue Danube." The owner, Virág, a man of fifty, recently won a large sum at the lottery. His lover, Ella, a pert young waitress with theatrical ambitions, promptly breaks up with her indigent fiancé, Barna, and rushes to cajole the ardent boss into divorcing his wife, Marianne, and marrying her instead. To save her endangered marriage, the clever wife works out a scheme with Barna to test whether Ella really loves her husband or only his money. She agrees to a divorce provided she gets all the money. The naive Virág consents, trusting that the waitress is unconditionally bewitched by his masculine appeal. Marianne meanwhile bequests

the whole amount to Barna with the proviso that he marry Ella
at once. The reconciliation proves rather easy and the ecstatic
couple soon leave for their honeymoon. When the penitent husband returns to his wife, she reveals what prompted her seemingly silly move: "Everything has its price. That was the price
tag the Almighty put on my happiness. Expensive, but worth
it" (220).

Scores of Molnár plays ridicule the corruptive effect of money,
as well as scurrilous, middle-aged husbands chasing fickle young
women and shrewd, manipulating wives emerging as ultimate
winners. In this play, the hero's power does not come from his
Samson-like hair but from his bankbook; when it is lost, due
to the altruistic betrayal of Delilah-Marianne, his magic is gone,
too. The familiar theme is treated with originality and winsome
humor.

Structurally faultless, the three-act comedy retains the comic
atmosphere throughout. The dialogue, vibrant with bons mots
and quirks, cleverly expounds the characterization. Marianne,
one of Molnár's most enchanting, positive heroines, is carefully
delineated: a brilliant, devoted woman who is willing to forego
wealth to keep her husband. In the end, she justifies her craftiness
by stating a typical Molnár paradox: "When my own happiness
is at stake, I'm cruel enough not to mind making someone else
happy" (220). One of the minor characters, Max, a brazen bar-
tender-busboy, eavesdrops, snoops about, and constantly butts
in to the conversations of the protagonists. This ubiquitous,
gossipy troublemaker, an older version of Józsi, greatly enhances
the play's comic impact.

In *Blue Danube* the author succeeds in realistically rendering
the social climate of the 1930s. In the microcosm of a restaurant,
different representatives of various social classes and their values
are viewed with gentle irony and accurate perception. Molnár's
unique dramatic ability helped to convert a mundane tale into
a sparkling, light comedy.

The production of the author's "swan-song" marked not only
the end of his reign on the European stages but also concluded
an era of peace and levity in which his effervescent histrionics
had entertained millions of people for almost four decades.

CHAPTER 6

Molnár's Masterpiece: Liliom

I Brief History

M OLNÁR'S best-known and most widely performed play,
Liliom, was originally written as a feuilleton entitled
"Bedtime Tale," in 1907. It was published the next year in his
short-story collection *Music*.¹ At the beginning of 1909, the
author expanded it into a play, writing almost uninterruptedly
for weeks on the balcony of the "Café New York." At its Budapest premiere at the Comedy Theater, December 7 that same
year, *Liliom* failed and closed after twenty-six performances.
Its major revivals in 1919, 1922, 1924, and 1937, however, met
enormous success. Since World War II, it has been performed
often and was broadcast on Hungarian radio and television.

Liliom became internationally known after its highly successful staging in Vienna in 1913.² However, the first English production in London in 1920 under the title *The Daisy* failed, although
its revival there in 1926 as *Liliom* fared better. The American
producers were reluctant to stage it for years, even though many
had options on it. Finally, the Theater Guild put it on at the
Garrick, on April 20, 1921, in the faithful adaptation of Benjamin Glazer.³ The play was received with unequivocal acclaim
and had 285 performances, featuring Joseph Schildkraut and Eva
Le Gallienne. The same couple revived it in 1932 at the Four-
teenth Street Theatre. Then, in 1940, another important revival
took place at the 44th Street Theatre, with Burgess Meredith
and Ingrid Bergman in the leading roles. Since then, the play
has been almost perennially revived in various repertories
in the USA.

It was first filmed as *A Trip to Paradise* in 1921 by Metro,
then in 1930 by Fox Film Corp. as *Liliom*. Its musical version,
Carousel, by Richard Rodgers and Oscar Hammerstein, opened

at the Majestic Theater on April 19, 1945, and ran 890 times. *Carousel's* movie version by 20th Century-Fox was released in 1956. The play has been translated into all major languages, including Turkish, Japanese, and Hindi. Both in Hungary and in the United States it has been reprinted many times and has been included in all major drama anthologies.[4]

II   *Legend or Self-Portrait?*

Unlike other genres, drama has not been ostensibly autobiographical. This is especially true of plays written at the turn of the century, but Molnár's plays often reflect his life. He was inextricably involved in the stage so that he could not help transposing his life and conflicts into his favorite medium. Although he claimed that in *Liliom* he had meant only to "dramatize a primitive legend of Budapest's 'lower depths,' relating it as naively as old women tell tales,"[5] his friends and many critics viewed it as his most subjective work, a naked self-analysis.

The play was written at the time when Molnár's marriage to Margi Vészi was disintegrating and the couple quarreled bitterly. The cafés bubbled with gossip about his cruel treatment of his family; he was rumored to have beaten not only his wife but his little daughter also. Molnár wrote *Liliom* to justify himself against these charges, and to appease his angry spouse by showing how even the rudest exterior might conceal a gentle nature, and how often people hurt those they love most. The play indeed may be viewed as a public atonement and a partial explanation of the author's occasional violent behavior. Thus, the repentant Molnár revealed his perverse love and paid a final, everlasting tribute of gratitude to Vészi for her endurance.

It was easy to identify Molnár as Liliom. Just like his hero, the author was cursed with a constitutional inability to avow love. He had a manifestly dual nature—a combination of extreme cruelty and genuine tenderness. Both characters suffered from an underlying feeling of inferiority and needed constant reassurance. Their inherent insecurity led to the use of a compensating mechanism: sadism, which was immediately followed by remorse and self-torture. Vacillating between love and abuse, doubt and defiance, arrogance and penitence, too stubborn to change, both men seemed insouciant, or perhaps unaware of the pain they inflicted by their almost pathologically egocentric behavior. When failures resulted, neither Molnár nor Liliom could accept inadequacy, and both resorted to suicide—although the author survived the attempt.

There were more concrete proofs of their similarity. Liliom was a barker and an innate musician; young Molnár, the gregarious social lion of the cafés, displayed much the same exhibitionism in his own milieu. In fact, sarcastically, he often called himself a barker,[6] and his attraction to music was also evident. But nothing speaks more eloquently about the kinship between the author and his hero than Molnár's epitaph. "Sleep, Liliom, my boy, sleep!" His third wife, Lili Darvas, who chose it for his tombstone, must have known!

Notwithstanding his seeming primitivism, the playwright's projected hero was so complex and neurotic that, as many of his literary predecessors, he was psychoanalyzed by experts.[7] Liliom's psychiatrist concluded his study by saying that the "sado-masochistic patient's brutality was a sublimation of his insecurity and maladjustment." The doctor looked upon *Liliom* as "a tragedy of souls unable to fit into a world of reality."[8] Of course, the play is a great deal more than that, and precisely in this "more" lies the universal theme of this legend.

III *Romance in the Slums*

The prologue is set in an amusement park on the outskirts of Budapest at the turn of the century. Liliom, a barker-bouncer for Mrs. Muskat's carousel, is cheerfully coaxing customers to buy tickets, shoving and pinching the girls. Julie, a simple servant, is fascinated by him but the proprietress chases her away in a fit of jealousy. Liliom stands up for her to Mrs. Muskat and gets fired as a result. Later that evening, Liliom finds Julie sitting under the blossoming acacia trees, and their love begins. Though she knows it will cost her her job, she stays with the barker and ignores the policemen's warning about her scoundrel partner.

Two months have elapsed; Liliom and Julie, now married, live in the shabby flat of her aunt, Mrs. Hollunder. Since he left the carousel, Liliom loiters, plays cards, and blusters, refusing any respectable employment. Julie endures his abuses and does the work for him. When the visibly frustrated idler finds out that his wife is pregnant, he rebuffs Mrs. Muskat, who now tries to lure him back to his old "position." The news of Julie's pregnancy fills Liliom with joy as well as worry. Since they need money for the baby, he succumbs to the suggestion of Ficsur, a petty criminal, that they rob a cashier.

Beneath the archway of a railroad embankment the thugs, while waiting for their intended victim, play cards, and Liliom loses his whole share of the loot. Soon the cashier appears and they accost him. But when he yells for help upon seeing the flashing knives, Ficsur twists away, and the inexperienced Liliom is caught in the act alone. Rather than go to jail, he stabs himself. Policemen carry him home on a stretcher, and his dying words reveal the contradictory nature that compelled him to hit his wife out of love: "Little Julie—I beat you—not because I was mad at you—no—only because I can't bear to see anyone crying" (128). Only when he is dead does Julie kneel at his side and whisper her farewell: "Sleep, Liliom, sleep you bad, quick-tempered, tough, unhappy, wicked-*dear* boy—sleep peacefully. . . . It was wicked of you to beat me—you bad boy, you—I love you" (131).

At this point, the naturalistic drama turns into fantasy. Two solemn-looking strangers lead the dead to the only kind of heaven Liliom can fathom: a celestial police court where suicides are being tried. There he learns that after purging himself for fifteen years in flames, he may be paroled for a day to visit his family and to redeem himself by a good deed.

In the last scene, the period of probation is over and Liliom arrives as a beggar at Julie's humble home. His sixteen-year-old daughter, Louise, turns from him when he tells her that her father was a bully. Liliom calls her back to offer his gift, a star he stole on his way. At her refusal to accept it, he slaps his child in helpless exasperation. The heavenly guards escort the incorrigible sinner to be confined "to fast in fires" eternally. Louise asks her mother why the blow struck by the stranger did not hurt. Julie understands and explains: "It has happened to me too . . . it is possible, dear,—that someone may beat you and beat you and beat you—and not hurt you at all . . ." (143).

Julie did not recognize Liliom; yet, her steadfast, loving heart is touched, perhaps supernaturally, by the same sympathetic chord that brought them together when he was alive. The power of her love sustains beyond death because only those die who are forgotten.

IV *Interpretation of the Theme*

Liliom is not only a brilliant examination of the unsoluble problem of who is worthy of redemption, but also a study of compassion and suffering; a thorough analysis of the relation of the created character to his family, society, and to his play-wright—the last by extension—may also reflect the relationship of man to God.

Because of such flexibility of meaning, the play offers numerous possibilities of interpretation. Most people consider it a tender, romantic love story, "as rarified and spiritual as the legend of Faust . . . in love spiritual democracy prevails so Gretchen and Julie are completely equal."[9]

Psychologists revel in pointing out the manifestation of how good and evil are inherent in man by analyzing the characters' paradoxical duality or neurotic behavior. Indeed, the play offers an intriguing subject for case studies. Since *Liliom* shifts from realism to fantasy, for some people it appears no more than a Hungarian folktale; for others, an allegory, a fable, or "a half drama, half mystery play with the local color typical of Budapest's contemporary underworld."[10]

The religiously oriented object to the author's sacrilegious treatment of eternal judgment. To some, the ending signifies the futility of a man predestined to damnation even though trying to save his soul. To others, such interpretation sounds contradictory since, after Liliom is given a chance of salvation, he seals his own fate by failing to perform even one good deed. On yet another level, the hero's derogatory references to Jews were interpreted as Molnár's cynical manipulation, a subtle way of fomenting anti-Semitism.[11]

Others, probing deeper, emphasize the play's sociological significance. For them it is a sad tale of a downtrodden, deprived couple destroyed by society, the tragedy of two simple people with a vision of what life should be. They are desperately trying, but fail to adjust to unyielding reality; hence their downfall. Thus, the play is also seen as a kind of weak protest against conformity. Molnár presents Liliom in such a manner that, though he has few redeeming qualities, he elicits admiration. He refuses to obey society's laws and vehemently rejects ordinary respectability. Consequently, many are puzzled: Is Liliom a disguised saint or a common criminal? Is his possible redemption meant symbolically or does it serve merely as a jibe?

Some Marxist literati criticize the author for not being more revolutionary, for his failure to be outspoken for the working class. According to them, Liliom is only a member of the lumpenproletariat and not a class-conscious industrial laborer whose similar plight would convey a more relevant social lesson.[12] The play indeed lacks dialectical tendencies. The more philosophical minded see *Liliom* as an acerbic satire of both the heavenly and earthly justice of the courts which brazenly discriminate against the poor.

Conjectures and hypotheses seem endless. The best interpretation, however, is offered by the playwright himself when Liliom utters his last words: "It's all the same to me who was right— It's so dumb. Nobody's right—but they all think they are right— A lot they know!" (129).

V   Criticism and Critiques

Several truly remarkable character portraits are given in *Liliom*. The dualistic hero, Andreas Zavoczki, is not a villain, only a maladjusted creature who ends up doing the wrong things in spite of all possible good intentions. This braggart dreamer is an obstinate nonconformist, a primitive person with a vicious temper, yet a noble man full of compassion. His ecstatic cry, "I'm going to be a father!" (114) is both that of a child's receiving a much-coveted toy, and of an archetypal man's joy over his virility and the promise of progeny. In the squalor of his drab existence, he remains an idealist and talks

with childlike naiveté about America, the novelty of the endless railroad, the thrill of a locomotive, and the mystery of the
telegraph wires. But he also acts as a brute, fierce and dangerous, when upset. He rebuffs pity, asks for no forgiveness, regrets
nothing, and wants to return to earth only "to wreak vengeance"
on Ficsur. While he adamantly refuses to turn into a respectable
"caretaker," he dies for his family and subliminally yearns for
his daughter's love and acceptance. This twenty-eight-year-old,
spontaneous, loud, passionate, macho man, who loves with dis-
arming simplicity all the little pleasures of life—women, gaiety,
music, beer, cigars, and his vocation—is Molnár's paradoxical
Everyman.

Julie, the eighteen-year-old, fragile, shy, uneducated peasant
girl, a "maid-of-all-work," is one of the author's most unforgettable heroines, who emerges as the eternal female ideal. She
loves unselfishly, with undemanding devotion and endurance.
With almost supernatural insight and common sense, she grasps
the realities of life and the true nature of her man. Demonstrating the finest ideals of love and wifehood, this simple
woman guides their married life with primordial intuition and
wins Liliom from the crafty Mrs. Muskat. She is taciturn and
inarticulate, but her farewell speech to her husband, inevitably
a soliloquy, is genuinely moving and poetic. Her character develops before us; through her love, the ignorant, passive Julie
metamorphoses into an epitome of wise womanhood. She learns
all that can be learned of the cruelty and beauty of life. Instead of marrying her suitor, a well-to-do, reliable carpenter
with whom she could enjoy comfort and stability, she remains
faithful to Liliom's memory and brings up her daughter alone,
working in a factory.

The minor characters—the flashy, devious Mrs. Muskat, the
sharp-tongued but kind-hearted Mrs. Hollunder, the sleek and
sinister Ficsur, the dull-witted but charming friend, Marie—
are similarly sharply drawn, realistic figures and aptly comple-
ment both the protagonists and the plot.

Liliom's structure, though loose, is crafted with boundless
inventiveness, energy, and flowing pictorial suggestiveness. By
changing the conventional division of acts into seven flexible
scenes, Molnár can maintain a fluent continuity of action. This

format ideally suits the rapid yet subtle shift from reality to fantasy, and permits the creation of a wholesome balance of climaxes and contrasts both in the entire play and within individual scenes. From the very beginning, he establishes the play's frequently alternating characteristics. Most scenes begin with casual realism and colloquial dialogues, then grow leisurely into imaginary realms, romance, or whimsical fancy: a police court in heaven or antics of reincarnation at the end.

Correspondingly, the dramatic motifs are also juxtapositions of the real and the fantastic, especially in the second part. In the celestial scene, where the action teeters breathlessly between tease and torment, among pink clouds and transcendental paraphernalia, the white-winged police-angels appear in traditional earthly uniforms and talk the *argot* of their mortal comrades. The other stage devices are also winsomely contrasted: the strident calliope music in the amusement park, the ethereal organ tune in heaven are underscored by the jolly chanting of the thieves' song. The clever and playful synthesis of realism and fancy makes the play titillating. But from the dramatic point of view, Benjamin Glazer felt that Molnár carried fantasy to the extremes here.[13] He says that it was too daring to kill the hero halfway through the play, then take him to heaven. Admittedly, it is difficult to make heaven credible on stage or anywhere else, yet it works here and seems "natural." The author had to have it to make his point: to explain Liliom's reincarnation which brings the bittersweet denouement.

The play oscillates between tragedy and comedy, sometimes bordering on melodrama. The style is similarly eclectic: highly poetic, symbolic, colloquial, grotesque, as well as sentimental, changing swiftly from episode to episode. The dialogue is pungent with idioms and the racy folksiness of the contemporary social classes it represents. The warm, emotional tone is interspersed with pathos, delicate irony, and rhapsodic passion. Carefully controlled comic relief is provided—the play permits laughter, but only occasionally and wryly; the humor is sardonic, evoking both delight and awe.

The play is designed as a legend, and legends tend to represent reality through the use of symbolism. Like the myth and fairy tale, *Liliom* is unusually rich in allusions and symbolism—also built on contrasts. The title, *Liliom*, both identifies and characterizes the hero in the contemporary vernacular. Paradoxically, it was common practice in the city's slums to apply the name of "lily," the white flower of innocence, to roughnecks. Therefore, Liliom's name *a priori* has symbolical significance: it suggests duality by connoting both fundamental goodness and brutality.

Other symbols further enhance the contrast. Red and white colors are abundant in the play. Liliom receives a red carnation, a flower-symbol of passion, from an admirer, but his heart is touched under the white acacia trees, the symbolic image of Julie's purity. She, on the other hand, unconsciously foresees her future as she speaks of the falling acacia blossoms, blown by the wind (106). Upon the railroad embankment there is a red and white signal flag, symbolizing the raging conflict within the hero: the red deed to be committed and the white state of inertia he has been in lately. His bloody death is caused by the very knife that has been used to cut their daily bread. The white star, a symbol of his repentance and Louise's innocence, is wrapped in a red handkerchief representing his punishment. In the celestial scene, a heavenly Magistrate, cloaked in a white robe, has gray hair and beard, and it is he who orders Liliom to be burned "in crimson fire" in order to purify his soul. Images of amber and candlelights, dying embers, shroud, white apron and table cloths richly support the mood. The merry-go-round, the only available means of transportation for the barker, goes nowhere; the train has a destination, and just before the crime Liliom gazes at the snorting engine with fascination. Later, however, he spits on it with resignation, indicating the futility of his imaginary trip; he knows he will never get away. Also suggestive is Julie's favorite carousel figure, the panther, the animal symbol for Liliom, who, as a barker, always wears black suits and "savagely" attacks his victims, the unsuspecting girls in the amusement park.

Because of its humane topic and profound beauty, *Liliom* won high praises from critics. The great German theater expert Alfred Kerr called it "undoubtedly a work of a genius," though adding that "it has an element of kitsch in it."[14] Among the Hungarian critics, Fenyő deserves attention. He lauded the play's lyric tone and stressed that its central theme was human rather than sociological. His conclusion ascertained that "with this drama Molnár left the camp of Bataille and joined Hauptmann's: the previous drawing-room comedy writer 'has graduated' into the group of true masters of fantasy."[15] Nagy is skeptical and decries *Liliom*'s "tear-jerking sentimentality," as well as "Julie's phony naiveté," but admires the author's sincerity and the striking dialogue and poignant characterization.[16] Endre Illés did not concur with his colleagues and hurled pejoratives and derogatory epithets on all aspects of the play, then missed the point to focus on the play's psychological significance when he wrote: "It is built on a mere soap-bubble idea ... its delivery sounds both mendacious and inartistic; this slum legend is like a ship run aground. ... Molnár's *apache* figures are false Hamsun reminiscences presented in the style of a café folklorist."[17]

The reception among the American critics was primarily positive. In Gassner's opinion, "*Liliom* is a play of rare beauty, one of the most gratifying romantic plays of the twentieth century."[18] Chandler deemed it a masterpiece "setting forth a truth universal."[19] Even Remenyi, who tends to be overly critical of Molnár, admitted that "the play is tender, touching and impressive ... a compound of ingeniousness, technique, inventive imagination expressed effectively, yet, on the whole a bit artificial."[20] Brooks Atkinson's review is concluded by stating that "*Liliom* is one of the most beautiful plays of our time, strange, exhilarating, original, and deeply moving."[21] The critics are still arguing, but *Liliom* does not seem to be fading because it has imperishable human and artistic values.

CHAPTER 7

Molnár in America

I Final Years

ON January 12, 1940, Molnár settled in New York's Plaza Hotel and spent his last twelve years in Room 835 of that simply furnished, book-filled abode, working almost uninterruptedly till his death. At first, he regarded his adopted country with fascination and made the adjustment to the New World with remarkable ease. Assisted by his dedicated secretary, Wanda Bartha, along with his wife, Lili Darvas, and numerous friends, Molnár diligently studied English, revised earlier works, and started new projects. In the summer, he ventured up to Lake Placid or spent his weekends at Montauk Point, L.I., among American colleagues and members of the Hungarian émigré colony. As years passed, and Hitler's atrocities became known, the author once more fell into deep depression alternating with high agitation. When in 1943 a massive heart attack compelled him to suspend work for a year, his mental condition grew even worse. When he gradually learned the tragic fate of Hungary and his Jewish friends, Molnár turned into a misanthrope. The once vain artist listened to reports about various openings of his plays with visible indifference, and resigned himself to the inevitable destiny of a man in exile. "We are all dead people, we refugees," he used to say, "we walk around, shadows among shadows, ghosts of what we were, in a world that does not know us and we only faintly comprehend."[1] In 1947, his apathy seemed to vanish temporarily when he received his American citizenship with ostensible pride and delight.

A few months after that, however, Mrs. Bartha's suicide dealt the heaviest blow upon him and seriously aggravated his frail mental and physical condition. After her death, Molnár really became a withdrawn, broken man. He buried himself in work,

157

apparently his only solace. During the last five years, he left his room only for his meals at a nearby Italian restaurant on 58th Street. He permitted only a few friends to visit him, and these were devastated by his puerile whimpering, frequent rages, and appearance. "This sad creature with cried-out, myopic eyes hardly resembled the old raconteur."[2] But the moribund septuagenarian author remained active and went on writing until his final collapse on March 22, 1952. After an unsuccessful operation, he died of cancer on April 1, 1952, in the Mount Sinai Hospital.

During these twelve years in exile, Molnár wrote and revised several novels, short stories, and plays. While none of these proved too successful, some were truly noteworthy. These last works, dripping with sentimentality on the surface and full of bitterness underneath, only rarely show evidences of his innate talent, perception, artistic sensibility, and wit. They sound like pathetic echoes of a glorious past, the sad residue of a rich life; in effect, mere therapeutic activities of a disillusioned old loner.

II   Autobiographical Prose

As Molnár's life reached its nadir, and the nostalgic longing for his homeland and the past reached its zenith, the author no longer made any conscious effort to disguise the autobiographical elements in his work. On the contrary, he seemed eager to disclose long-concealed events of his life and to expose his emotions and views more sincerely than ever before. Unfortunately, this urge for self-revelation happened at a time when his artistry and reputation were alike in a decline.

The first prose work of the new immigrant, The Blue-Eyed Lady,[3] stands alone in this period of self-search. It is a short, melancholy fairy tale about two orphans. At Christmas time, their dead mother manipulates a mannequin in a store window, making it her double, and through the puppet she comforts her children from heaven. The idea for the book came to Molnár during his daily walk by a high-fashion store in the vicinity where he watched the holiday displays. This fairly successful juvenile tale is the last proof of the writer's intimate knowledge of children.

Farewell My Heart was the first Molnár novel to appear originally in English and be translated into Hungarian afterwards.[4] The story, narrated by a Hungarian journalist on his deathbed in a New York hospital, was allegedly based on the life of the author's old friend Loránt Barabás. In reality, however, it is a transparent autobiographical fragment only peripherally relating to Molnár's model.[5]

The protagonist meets Edith Gaal, a pretty dancer, on a refugee ship sailing for New York at the end of 1939—the same time Molnár did. The girl, thirty years younger, offers her love to the aging journalist, who is overwhelmed, but, following his common sense, resists the temptation. When they land, however, he can no longer control his passion and rushes into her hotel room, whereupon he suffers a heart attack. Edith nurses him back to life—as Wanda did Molnár. To save the weak man from further excitement, the dancer departs for Hollywood. During convalescence, he meets a wealthy, middle-aged widow and marries her. But "the virgin temptress"—as Edith calls herself—returns, and finally the lovers unite. At the end of a rapturous week together, the hero has another seizure. As he lies dying, dictating his memoirs, Edith flirts with his physician. The postscript notes that she eventually marries the doctor.

This mundane, inane story embodies the familiar theme of an aging man's anguished infatuation with a much younger woman, and also the choice between life and death. The treatment offers nothing novel except a few reminiscences of the author's own voyage to America and the story of his first heart attack. Otherwise, the book is totally devoid of originality and grace. It fails to read as a tragic confession of a humiliated man forced into exile; instead, it sounds like a pretentious cry of self-pity uttered by a lovelorn old roué.

Molnár had a great deal of difficulty in coming to terms with any disaster. Thus, the novel reads like a cynically private story taking place in a historical vacuum at a time when Europe was burning, millions were massacred, and the characters themselves were victims of the upheaval. Molnár's artistic and social conscience appears dormant. As Lukács, perhaps too severely, remarked, "In those days, only an immoral opportunist or a rebellious surrealist could ignore the era or use the events as mere backdrops in his writing."[6] Indeed, Molnár was never quite at ease with himself as a purveyor of calamities, but he did portray some ominous facts: the encroaching dangers, escaping Jews, constant passport controls, anti-Semitic harassment, and crowded refugee camps. But these phenomena had little to do with the characters or the basic theme. When the hero talks with Edith about love, he "thought of the blood-stained Poles lying in the ditches beside highways,"[7] and turned solemn momentarily. This and similar comments appear occasionally in parentheses. The author's ostrichlike attitude toward the dismal happenings is best summed up in the protagonist's remark, made after the suicide of his Jewish doctor: "This event was a fact, but for me it would continue forever to be a monstrous lie, like so many other things which happened since 1939."[8]

The style is languid, mechanical, almost overly controlled, as if the writer were deliberately withholding his true emotions: the descriptions lack vitality and perception; the dialogues are trite and flaccid, fraught with banalities. The main characters are histrionic and unconvincing, and so is the plot. Some well-sketched minor characters and a few poignant observations seem insufficient to redeem this essentially insipid novel which went virtually unnoticed in 1945.

Unfortunately, Molnár's other novel, published in the same year, also failed to attract attention. *The Captain of St. Margaret's* is a highly polished extended version of a lengthy short story, "The Pillar of Steam," written in 1926, about the life of a flamboyant, swashbuckling, braggart cavalry officer,[9] who entertains his fellow Bohemians with highly exaggerated tales of his fantastic adventures on Margaret Island. This colorful novel, which represents the author at his narrative best, incorporates several early sketches, dialogues, and feuilletons.

Incontestably, *Companion in Exile* is Molnár's most dolorous and depressing work.[10] This final tribute to Mrs. Bartha was written immediately after her suicide in 1947. Fundamentally, the book is another pathetic story of an old man's tragic love and a swansong of remorse. This loosely constructed autobiographical elegy reveals most eloquently the author's dual nature: his merciless cynicism and soaring sentimentality. It was designed to serve a double purpose: to register his grieving thoughts and psychological reaction to Wanda's death in the form of a self-therapeutic diary; and to reward the loyal companion with a belated, lasting memento. Regrettably, the lachrymal labor presents Wanda in a rather unsavory light; she emerges as a generous and devoted but somewhat superficial woman who enjoys nothing more than meeting celebrated people in the shadow of her idol. As the last Muse of the genius, she endures his vicious moods and vilification like a martyr, but when his egomania and sadism begin to run amuck, she escapes into suicide. Molnár's jeremiads, too, reverberate insincerity, especially the laments over his cruel treatment of her.

Companion in Exile is arranged in thirteen chapters; in the first seven the bereaved author describes Wanda's death, delineates her character, and tearfully reminisces about the happy times they spent together. The longest part, Chapter 8, includes in their entirety the unchanged daily logs Wanda had kept for decades, depicting the festive Molnár openings and their luxurious travels, always listing encounters with famous people.[11] When the entries about him do not seem complimentary enough, Molnár makes corrections in parentheses or adds his comments in a self-promoting fashion. For instance, when Wanda mentions the master's first attempt at writing an autobiography, Molnár writes: "Let me remark here that it is called *Farewell My Heart,* published by Simon and Schuster in New York in 1945."[12] Chapters 9–12 contain brief episodes from their life in America, explain their work routine, and include several imaginary dialogues with the dead woman.

The last chapter is a painful, almost incoherent monologue which tries to canonize his lost companion. The final eulogy takes the form of a hallucinatory scene from "a scribbled, fragmentary, confused, never-to-be written, still-born play, called *Night Nurse.*"[13] A man (Molnár) is dying and his nurse (Wanda) —an angel who descends from heaven—dies of a broken heart in her sleep. Then a clerk (Jesus) comes to take her back "to the place from which she so rebelliously longed to depart, from which (not even knowing why) she desired so irresistibly to come down to earth."[14] The genuine sorrow, tenderness, and

simple, moving repentance in the last chapter ring true and
evoke pity.

The book was prepared in an unorthodox fashion. The author
wrote in Hungarian, then he read the completed pages in German every other day to a bilingual American, Barrows Mussey,
who jotted down each sentence in English, working as a simul-
taneous translator. Hence the book's uneven style, admitted even
by Molnár, who called it a "literary mixed salad." In addition
to its lack of unity, the book is redundant, unpolished, and often simplistic. The loquacious descriptions are frequently interrupted by trivial asides, while the rambling self-analyses smack
of self-delusion and pseudopsychology. They unveil Molnár's
chaotic transcendentalism, paranoid fears, snobbery, supersti-
tiousness, egotism, and overwhelming vanity. Despite its numerous artistic flaws, this odd memoir, the most significant writing
he did after Wanda's death, is a valuable literary evidence
of the profound changes Molnár and his art had undergone
during the fifteen years spent with Wanda. This ironical finale
stands as a sad document of a sinking mind and a life gone
astray: the true son of Budapest subsisting in an alien environment, the stage-prophet of love living in an emotional vacuum,
realizing that he has been incapable of establishing even one
sustaining, genuine, loving relationship. The long awaited autobiographical notes contain little new facts or information. Consequently, the book received very unsympathetic reviews and
sold only a few copies.

III   *Plays of Loneliness*

Molnár's last theater pieces reflect a man at the end of his
tether—a stage veteran around whom the last props of the dramatic edifice have crumbled and who, with an obsession for
carrying on, tries to stamp his feet on the last remaining bricks.
To be sure, his manic insistence on writing was not motivated
by pursuit of money or fame, since he had both. For him playwriting was the most satisfactory outlet for his emotions, the
easiest vehicle to convey his opinions. It is not surprising, therefore, that these late confessional dramas were pervaded by
characteristics of a despondent old age: a mixture of sadness

melancholy, pathos, and resignation. Moreover, these plays tend to be at one and the same time more sentimental and ostensibly more dedicated to edifying moral purposes. It appears that the gradually estranged playwright no longer sought only to entertain; instead, he began moralizing—a feat rather alien to his nature. Nevertheless, the deteriorating dramatist still managed to produce some pieces worthy of listing in the annals of literature.

The King's Maid, a symbolic tragedy of faith, was first conceived in the mid 1920s, together with its twin play, *Miracle in the Mountain,* containing the same setting and theme. In 1941, upon Wanda's insistence, Molnár finished it, but her favorite play was a dead flop and quickly closed in two American repertory theaters.[15] The playwright later explained the circumstances of the play's failure.

I started writing this play four years before the German murder of Jews. After it had been rewritten, translated, rehearsed, and given two tryouts, we all saw quite plainly, under the pressure of events rushing far more swiftly than we, that the play ought obviously be shelved for good.[16]

The plot is simple. Rosenbaum, a destitute, sickly, orthodox Jewish peddler in his late seventies, buys a sackful of discarded books one day. Back at home in the dilapidated rooming house, his only friend, Orphan Ann, a deeply religious, wretched little servant, searches the bag and finds a Bible. Enthusiastically, she begins reading and explaining it to her friend. As Rosenbaum becomes acquainted with the New Testament, he gradually goes through a transformation and falls in love with Jesus and His teachings. Unfortunately, however, he is 2,000 years too late. After Ann's jealous friend beats him fatally, the old man forgives the assault and tells the police that he injured himself by an accidental fall. Then, in the arms of the "King's maid," he dies happily, quoting from the Sermon on the Mount.

Professing faith and the victory of virtue over evil, this pathetic drama also shows what a deep impact the story of Jesus had on the playwright during his depression in 1936. The characters are realistic, and Molnár's old technical skill is still apparent, but the tenuous plot is unconvincing, and the dialogues are both deflated and sanctimonious, aiming at cheap effects.

By and large the same criticism applies to his next play, . . . Or Not To Be, a little-known melodrama, existing only in manuscript form and never performed anywhere.[17] This painfully overwrought play elaborates on the frustrated love affair between an old, rich industrialist, Kristov, and his tubercular secretary, Irene. Choosing to die with dignity, even if in squalor, the proud girl leaves her lover and marries a poor young clerk as her condition worsens. She does not want to become a kept woman recuperating in a Swiss sanatorium at Kristov's expense. When Irene's fate becomes known, Kristov, a heartbroken, lonely man, turns to God as he withers away, tormented by remorse. The pretentious, inane action moves sluggishly and delivers nothing even remotely interesting.

Far more ambitious and polished is Molnár's other play, Waxwork, or Panoptikum, released in 1941. This revised version of the 1940 comedy Merciless Mrs. Roy ran fairly successfully in German and Austrian theaters.[18] Its English translation by Arthur Richman has never been staged, but was included in Romantic Comedies. As in The Swan and Olympia, Molnár satirizes haughty and hypocritical aristocrats, but he also intends "to deride those drawing-room plays which fawningly glorified these people as demigods throughout half a century."[19]

This fantasy-farce begins with a prologue, set in the present. The manager-guide of a wax museum leads a group of visitors into a dimly lit baroque room representing Austrian imperial glory, and introduces the eleven wax figures standing in a semicircle. Their story is revealed as the lights go on and the figures come to life. The action takes place at the Austrian embassy in Rome, at the turn of the century. Princess Ann, the young, arrogant, irreproachable wife of the middle-aged, disdainful ambassador, Prince Kron-Leithen, is tormented by shame over falling in love like any mortal woman and, alas, with a commoner. Her paramour is the thirty-five-year-old house architect, Robert Thomas. The icy goddess is so attracted to him physically that she summons her lawyer to file for a divorce. The prince is about to accept Ann's decision, when it turns out that Robert is an agent of the Russian Secret Service. His contact-

boss is none other than the ambassador's head lackey, Diegelman, a crafty man, also in love with the princess. The police
raid the architect's abode and find incriminating documents.
Ann's fate is sealed; since she is a distant relative of the Emperor, she will be destroyed. But Diegelman saves her from
disgrace by revealing that it was he who smuggled the papers
into Robert's place to prevent the wedding and to mislead the
Italians, whom he despises. Social tragedy is thus averted. After
the relieved prince grants his consent, Ann is free to marry
Thomas. At the end, on the slowly darkening stage, the members of the cast take their semicircular position to greet the
Italian king, who has been announced, and freeze into wax
figures.

Thematically, Molnár again unleashes his social criticism
through parodying supercilious, overbearing, high-class society,
but his tone here is more subdued, his critical thrust less pierc-
ing than in previous plays. He presents these superior creatures
as caricatures, proving that they were not human beings but wax
figures even in their own lifetime. The dramatic conflict and its
solution are almost identical with those in *Olympia*, except that
the resolution in this play leads to a happy misalliance.

The comic effect is achieved through the artificial, elabo-
rately sublime language and ceremonious, ridiculously solemn
behavior of the aristocracy. Members of the royalty emerge as
calculatedly exaggerated stereotypes, but Thomas, the outsider,
is not as compassionately portrayed and compelling as his
Hungarian predecessors, Ági and Captain Kovacs. This romantic
parody, reminiscent of the old Molnáresque ingenuity, dry humor, and verbal sparkling, is the best comic piece of this period.

The Emperor or *The Last Role*, Molnár's last tragedy of
terror and passion, was copyrighted in 1942, but its revised
English text by Arthur Richman was released only years later.[20]
On April 20, 1946, the play was presented in Budapest at the
rebuilt Comedy Theater, marking the last opening of a new
Molnár play in Hungary. There, unfortunately, it received unfairly harsh notices; in America it has never been published
or staged.

The tragic tale unfolds in 1804 during the Napoleonic terror.
In a Paris theater, actors are preparing for the performance of

Racine's *Andromaque*. The leads are played by the legendary actor couple—who have been passionately in love for seventeen years—Desroses and his wife, Amelie. The actress is disturbed because their beloved only son, Armand, has disappeared. When they learn that the boy was executed as a rebel, Amelie collapses, goes insane with grief, and the show is canceled. Meanwhile, the police are alerted to arrest the whole company for treason. They all escape, except the bereaved couple. Amelie is seized by the idea of revenge: she wants to lure the emperor into her bed and kill him. Desroses, a superb actor, fulfills his adored wife's last demented wish and appears as Napoleon. He plays the role faultlessly, and after a fascinating seduction scene, he is stabbed fatally by his wife. The police storm in and at first believe that the man lying there in the emperor's uniform is Napoleon himself, until an old actress, who had witnessed the tragedy in hiding, identifies the famous Desroses. The captain then declares him a national hero, since he assumes that the actor pretended to be Napoleon to prevent the latter's assassination and thus died for the emperor.

Through this haunting tragedy Molnár voiced a strong protest against tyranny and a desperate outcry against any kind of oppression, whether it was Napoleon's or Hitler's. In addition, the well-honed plot embodied a variation on his favorite theme about actors. As he showed in *The Guardsman* and *Marshall*, a born Thespian never stops acting; when tragedy strikes in real life, and even when facing death, a true actor plays his assigned role, because for him "the play's the thing" forever. Learning his son's fate, Desroses remonstrates about this curse: "It's a terrible profession, my friends. It's no longer possible for me to see people without thinking of them as audience. I, who was famous for weeping heart-breaking tears on the stage—although I was the happiest man on earth—I don't know how to face *real* tragedy.... It seems that as an actor I've faced too many pretended ones ... but they were all only memorized."[21]

All of its characters are convincing and well developed. The two main ones especially offer memorable roles for great actors. The dialogues are fluid and the highly symbolical language is ably supported by appropriate quotes from Racine. The impeccably constructed three acts repeatedly exhibit the author's fine technical skills. Admittedly, the tone is often filled with pathos and there is an awesome deliberateness about the play, bordering on overelaboration. In general, however, *The Emperor* is far superior to scores of celebrated Molnár plays written in the preceding fifteen years.

In 1946, the Hungarian critics received the play squeamishly; they admitted its "noble intentions, superb technique and poetic style," but criticized its basic premise and the action for being "too sensational, vying for cheap effects like a murder mystery."[22] This reaction might have been politically motivated. *The Emperor* indeed deserves an objective revaluation.

Wedding Day, or *Nuptial Song*, on the other hand, is a jejune, depressingly poor, unfunny comedy.[23] Dick Esmond, a noted old actor, announces his marriage to his eighteen-year-old secretary, Mary. But his lawyer intervenes, disclosing that the bride is Dick's own daughter born after he separated from his wife, the now twice-divorced Lady Dilford. He also learns that the girl, though starstruck, is secretly in love with a young man. The shocked but touched father quickly marries Mary off to her sweetheart. At the wedding Dick meets his former wife and discovers that he still loves her, and also that Mary is in fact not their child. The deceitful conspiracy has been arranged and financed by Lady Dilford with her own romantic interest in mind,—which does, after all, triumph. Recovered from the startling revelation, and after meeting his real daughter, the ecstatic actor happily sings his own nuptial song. The improbable, contrived tale, delivered in pedestrian, weary style, in crawling dialogues, hardly bears Molnár's signature.

Following his heart attack in 1943, the playwright related his medical history and the plights of cardiac patients in a hastily drafted melodrama, *Noah's Ark*. Later, he revised it into a comedy, *Pit-a-Pat*, which was finally adapted by P. G. Wodehouse as *Game of Hearts*. Despite the authors' reputation, this situation comedy has never been staged in English, but it saw print in 1952.[24]

Briefly, the story is as follows: the fifty-five-year-old Vincent Reid, a fabulously wealthy retired test pilot, is advised by his New York physician, Dr. Moore, that he has a serious heart ailment. To survive, he must settle down to a quiet life and avoid excitement. During his visits, Linda, the young nurse, displays ostensible interest in the melancholy, lonely patient. In search of a permanent home, Vincent locates his old love, Sophie, who twenty-three years ago married another man while carrying Vincent's child. She now manages a rooming-house and lives with one of her tenants, Clem. To find domestic tranquillity and to provide for his newly found son, Dick, Vincent rents a room in Sophie's house. When Clem learns that the intruder is Dick's father, he takes out his revolver and starts shooting at the ceiling, insane with jealousy. The scene and the emotional turmoil aggravates Vincent's condition but he is still adamant "to have a family at last." Finally, Sophie and her household agree to his moving in, provided he makes a new will leaving them all of his fortune. Deeply disappointed, Vincent departs, returns to the doctor and proposes to Linda. A dramatic somersault ensues: the cold, professional Dr. Moore, totally unexpectedly, expresses his love for Linda, to the nurse's utter bewilderment. She sides with the boss, her longtime idol, and the unlucky, twice-rejected hero resigns himself to assisting Linda in taking a sample of the doctor's blood required for the marriage certificate.

The tragicomic twist at the end concludes a trivial, tired, incongruous story in which the dramatic conflict remains unresolved: Vincent multiplied rather than solved his problems. The listless and unsavory characters are cardboard figures and their dialogues sound empty and witless. Molnár also failed to project his intended social criticism about the greed and pettiness of the American middle class. Instead, he simply transferred his own fear of death, bitterness, and mistrust into his hero, doing even that rather unconvincingly. *Game of Hearts* shows that the comic spirit and creative vein had irrevocably dried out in the master of comedy.

The final proof of this is Molnár's last completed comedy found among his papers by Lili Darvas after his death. Though undated, *There Is a Play Tonight* was most likely written during the early 1940s.[25] In 1961, Darvas made an attempt to stage it in America, but the play failed ignominiously.[26] Resembling *Great Love*, it revolves around the two Peter sisters, who are as different in nature as they are alike in beauty. Dorothy, a budding playwright, is temperamental and self-assured, while Eva is a serene introvert. When the play, set in Vienna in the 1930s, opens, Dorothy discovers that her sister is secretly in love with George, a reputed Don Juan, about to be engaged to a silly friend. Eva's plight captures Dorothy's creative fancy; she vows to turn the young man's affection toward her sister by writing a play. She transmutes the real situation into a melodrama acted out by the very people who are involved in the events—except George, who is assigned as a critic and audience. His part is played by an actor friend, Charles. During the intense rehearsals, George falls in love with the energetic playwright, and Eva with Charles. George confesses his love and tells Dorothy that he has known all along what the scheme was. Thus, she failed as a good fairy-dramatist but succeeded in procuring husbands for both of them. While some echoes of the earlier Molnár can be heard, the play lacks spirit and substance.

IV   *Unfinished Manuscripts*

Molnár left five unfinished plays and several filmscripts behind; sketches and synopses of these were found in the office of his New York agent, Dr. Edmond Pauker.[27] Most of them bear no dates, but they were all written in America and translated into English. These incomplete pieces—discussed in assumed chronological order often based on sheer deduction—are fundamentally uningenious and superficial but still show comic possibilities, and a few would have been worthy of completion. Only brief synopses of these unfinished plays are listed without critical commentary.

The first draft for *Girl of My Dreams*, a variation of *Riviera*, was prepared in 1941. A few years later, after Molnár had completed the manuscript, it was translated by various people. One version was eventually sold as a television script.[28] It features two young lovers working in a dress shop: Bob, a penniless, romantic window-designer, mourns the loss of his girl friend, the model Janet, to a rich customer. For consolation, Bob seats the girl's wax figure at the dinner table every night and talks to the mannequin. One day his dreams come true: the real Janet returns and takes the place of her replica for good.

The Empress has a clever outline for a comedy in three acts, but only a few scenes were written. At the end of the last century, a young upholsterer apprentice falls in love with Elisabeth, Empress of Austria, while working on the Emperor's bedroom. Several years later, the by then well-to-do painter, still consumed by his mad obsession, sees a play about the empress in Paris. The actress portraying Elisabeth shows such a remarkable likeness to his idol that he decides to "buy" her. For a large fee, she is asked to continue playing the part of the empress in real life, for him alone. She consents and eventually marries her crazy benefactor, who by that time is just as happy as if he had conquered the real empress.

The *Smile of a Woman*, or *Bill Duval*, is a fragment of a comedy about an idealistic, honest journalist, Bill Duval, who gets himself arrested and jailed under self-fabricated charges. He is determined to unveil the rampant corruption of the local legal authorities by going through the system and examining it from within. The document proving his innocence, however, is deliberately misplaced by an intimidated officer. After long court battles, the document is mysteriously found, but it is his girl friend's beguiling smile that leads to his release. He marries his "liberator" and becomes famous after the shocking articles are published.

Only the synopsis and a brief scene were completed of a comedy, *Stella* or *Yvonne*, which, according to Molnár's notes, was based on facts. A young divorcée with an alert seven-year-old son is planning to marry a rich French aristocrat, Roger. But her ex-husband, Frank, a noted pianist, suddenly shows up at the castle. During the mother's absence he had been hired by Roger as a music teacher for the little boy, who seems to have inherited his father's talent. By the time Stella returns, the child has grown so attached to his teacher that his affection eventually leads to the reunion of the disrupted family. Happily, they leave the estate to start a new life together.

Jewels for Milady is a fragment of a comedy about a wealthy Paris gambler who presents his lover with fabulous jewels, but when he goes broke he retrieves them in a novel fashion. In disguise, he stages a holdup at gunpoint and robs her of all the jewelry. The girl turns the robbery into a prank and thus saves him from jail. They get married and from then on he repeats the game of playing bandit from time to time.

With a few exceptions, the entire dramatic output of the final years is anticlimactic and attenuated. In accordance with his dual nature, Molnár's opinion of his geriatric work is typically ambivalent. For one thing, he cynically scorns his critics and fanatically—or cravenly—adheres to his self-delusion of greatness. Yet, he admits his declining talent and stoops to degrading, sentimental excuses, seeking pity and understanding. What can be a more fitting critical evaluation of the last phase of Molnár's dramatic career than the playwright's own woebegone self-analysis:

One may see in these works how tragedies and time have affected the mind of a writer who had so long punctiliously striven to appear a professional dramatist, and has followed so religiously the technical rules of his many-thousand-year-old profession that he has always drawn his loudest critical jeers for this very reason. . . . No writer before me has ever published such morbid jumble, which on both commercial and literary grounds belongs to nowhere but in the ashcan. Yet there may be someone who will understand after reading them why in this period I cannot withstand the compulsion to write . . . and perhaps in these confused scribblings certain imponderables may be sensed that are missing from what I have done before.[29]

CHAPTER 8

Conclusion

"*MOLNÁR!* Author, stage-director, dramatist, poet: Ferenc Molnár. Today, whether at home in his beloved Hungary, or here, in America, a name to reckon with."[1] Thus exclaimed David Belasco in 1929, echoing many other critics around the world. Through his plays, Molnár broke out of the literary isolation of his native land, and achieved international fame by amusing audiences everywhere for five decades. Instead of pretending to convey social messages or extreme profundity, this prolific, facile, imaginative writer aimed merely to entertain by transforming his personal experience into effective works of art.

Molnár had no significant links with any fashionable literary movements of his time; he stood alone, but dipped freely into the literary wealth of the past. He utilized the tenets of Naturalism, Neo-Romanticism, Expressionism, and the Freudian psychoanalytical concepts, but only when and insofar as they suited his purpose. In his prose, he was inspired by the works of Zola, Maupassant, Dumas, Tolstoy, and Dostoevsky. In his dramas, he at first continued the tradition of the French boulevard authors—Capus, Bataille, Bernstein, and Bernard; later, Wilde, Shaw, Hauptmann, Schnitzler, and Pirandello left the deepest impression upon him. By fusing the realistic narrative and stage tradition of Hungary with Western influences into a cosmopolitan amalgam, Molnár emerged as a versatile artist whose style was uniquely his own.

As a Hungarian journalist, he valued keen observation, precise description, suave mischief, and wit. His easy-flowing, urbane, vibrant short stories are poetic and meticulously structured, reflecting his consummate skill with dialogue. Although his novels are characterized by stylistic brilliance and cleverly calculated plots, thematically their range is rather narrow, and

172

in content largely empirical. While his mostly autobiographical novels are only interesting period pieces, *The Paul Street Boys* emerges as a masterpiece.

Molnár, a natural-born playwright, demonstrated mesmerizing, unerring dramatic instincts, originality, dazzling technique, and craftsmanship, and it was in this field that he rendered his major contribution. In his graceful, whimsical, sophisticated drawing-room comedies, he provided a felicitous synthesis of Naturalism and fantasy, Realism and Romanticism, cynicism and sentimentality, the profane and the sublime. He delivered his invariably interesting plots with accurate dramatic timing, through witty, sparkling, and spicy dialogues. According to Robert Brustein, his civilized plays enjoy universal appeal because of their "champagne quality: they are healthy, bubbly, and refreshing; they suit the taste of a general public everywhere."[2] Molnár wrote elegant, satiric dramas on manners, human frailties, and illusions; he portrayed suave, lovesick gentlemen and perfumed, cunning women, or thugs and simple servants, all engaged in the battle of the sexes. Out of his forty-two plays, *The Devil*, *Liliom*, *The Swan*, *The Guardsman*, and *The Play's the Thing* endure as recognized classics of the world of drama.

His artistry shines most brightly in his technique. He was an undisputed expert of stagecraft. The inextricable fusion of his life with the theater gave him theatrical versatility and vast knowledge of all the tricks of the stage. The ease and vigor of his innovative talent, the ability to construct plays faultlessly, the discipline and sense of dramatic proportion, make him one of the finest theatrical craftsmen of his era.

He once stated that he wrote only what was natural to him. Perhaps that is why his work was enormously successful during and after his life, both with the simple reader or audience and knowledgeable critics. He is superb as an observer, a technician, a storyteller, and a humorist. He does not conceal his ideas in obscure language, pseudosymbolism, forced social consciousness, or intellectual aloofness. His brilliance is one that not only entertains but also enlightens.

His tremendous national and international fame inspired scores of Hungarian playwrights—Elemér Boross, László Fodor, Lajos Biró, László Bús-Fekete, Ernő Vajda, Attila Orbók, and

Imre Földes, among others—to follow his style of playwriting. The export plays of these perhaps not always conscious imitators achieved temporary success abroad, especially in the United States, but their popularity died rapidly. The interest in Molnár's work, however, has not abated. His place in the world of drama is secure—most of his plays are still relevant and are being performed all over the world.

Molnár's long and turbulent life was one of hard and incessant work. For over fifty years he transposed his inner conflict into his literary work; writing was his oxygen, elixir, and self-therapy. Though not all his creations are masterpieces, few are carelessly done. He wanted primarily to be an entertainer, not a preacher or propagandist. He succeeded. By his special skill, he provided the public with escape, gaiety, and an illusory world in which conflicts were fun and amenable to solution. Perhaps not a Hungarian Molière, but certainly a Hungarian Noel Coward, Molnár deserves respect as a stage magician who, "with a flourish, lifted us up to the sky."[3] A true artist, he contributed prodigally to the literary heritage of the world by spreading truth and joy among his fellow men.

Notes and References

Chapter One

1. For a detailed history of Hungary see: Ferenc Eckhart, *A Short History of the Hungarian People* (London, 1931); Denis Sinor, *History of Hungary* (London, 1959); Paul Ignotus, *Hungary* (New York, 1972).

2. For more details see: Robert A. Kann, *The Habsburg Empire: a Study in Integration and Disintegration* (New York, 1957).

3. In 1917 the following minorities lived in Hungary proper: descendants of German settlers: 1,901,043; Croatians: 181,882; Slovaks: 1,946,165; Rumanians: 2,948,049; and approximately 1 million of other races. Louis K. Birinyi, *The Tragedy of Hungary* (Cleveland, 1924), p. 197.

4. Prime Minister of Hungary between 1903–1905; he was recalled to power in 1913, resigned in 1917. Son of Kálmán Tisza, Prime Minister of Hungary between 1875–1890.

5. Paul Ignotus, *Hungary* (New York, 1972), p. 77.

6. Béla Kun, Marxist ex-prisoner of war, participated in the Russian Revolution and had been operating under Lenin's guidance.

7. Before the Peace Treaty, Hungary's population had been 18,264,533; as a result of the new boundaries 59 percent, 10,782,576 people, were severed from her. Hungary lost 68 percent of her land; all salt deposits and natural gas; 99 percent of iron mines; 60 percent of heavy industry; 90 percent of timber and wool industry; 73 percent of cotton industry. Birinyi, p. 204.

8. Ignotus, p. 126.

9. Between 1890–1900 the population of Budapest grew by more than half. *Budapest székesfőváros statisztikai évkönyve 1899–1901* (Budapest, 1902), p. 490.

10. Molnár was born Neumann. His change of name was a gesture of patriotic assertation; he felt he could not write under a German name: it would be unfair to Hungarian literature. Molnár means "miller" in Magyar: this was the profession of his favorite uncle. S. N. Behrman, *The Suspended Drawingroom* (New York, 1965), p. 193.

11. In 1910, 8.5 percent of the total population was Jewish; 7 percent lived in the cities, mostly in Budapest. Ignotus, p. 91.

12. Ignotus, p. 92.

13. Joseph Held, "Young Hungary: The *Nyugat* periodical, 1908–1914," *East European Monographs*, No. XI (New York and London, 1975), p. 272.

14. Antal Szerb, *Magyar Irodalomtörténet*, 2nd ed. (Budapest, 1935), II, p. 426.

15. The contributors included Zoltán Ambrus, Jenő Heltai, Zoltán Thury, Ernő Osvát, Ignotus (Hugó Veigelsberg), and Molnár.

16. For a list, see Zoltán Horváth, *Magyar századforduló*, 2nd ed. (Budapest, 1974). Some outstanding figures in music: Béla Bartók and Zoltán Kodály; in art: Gyula Benczur, Pál Szinyey-Merse, Béla Iványi-Grünwald; in psychology: Sándor Ferenczi; in science: Oszkár Jászi, Gyula Pikler, and Ottó Herman.

17. Péter Nagy, "The Literary Revolution in Hungary around 1900," *New Hungarian Quarterly*, 18, No. 67 (1977), 130–31. The editors of the *Nyugat* were Ernő Osvát and Miksa Fenyő; the contributors included the best poets and prose writers, among them: Endre Ady, Mihály Babits, Dezső Kosztolányi, Margit Kaffka, György Lukács, Oszkár Jászi, and Zsigmond Móritz.

18. The Thália Society (1904–1908) was organized by noted theatrical experts; Sándor Hevesi (director of the National Theater), László Bánóczi, György Lukács and Marcel Benedek (drama critics). The society trained actors and reorganized outmoded stage techniques.

Chapter Two

1. John Gassner, *Masters of the Drama* (New York, 1945), p. 41.

2. Behrman, p. 196.

3. Benjamin Glazer, Preface, *Liliom* (New York, 1921), p. XI.

4. Behrman, p. 202.

5. Gassner, p. 479.

6. Győző Hajdu, "Elhervadt-e a *Liliom?*" *Műhely* (Bucharest, 1967), p. 359.

7. Molnár, Preface, *Csendélet* (Budapest, 1925), p. I.

8. Molnár, *Companion in Exile*, trans. Barrows Mussey (New York, 1950), p. 141.

9. Molnár, "Preface," *Színházi Élet* 6, No. 52, (1917), p. 1.

10. After her divorce from Molnár, Margit Vészi became a literary celebrity; as a distinguished reporter, she traveled widely and in the 1920s married an Italian Baron, Paolo Montica. She came to the USA before World War II, and in 1961 she committed suicide

11. Frank W. Chandler, *Modern American Playwrights* (New York, 1931), p. 442.

12. Behrman, p. 248.

13. *Ibid.*, p. 250.

14. After World War I Andor Miklós launched several newspapers and became the owner of Hungary's largest printing corporation, Athenaeum, Molnár's major publisher till World War II.

15. *Theatre*, three one-act plays (1921), *Heavenly and Earthly Love* or *Launzi* (1922), *The Red Mill* or *Mima* (1923), and *The Glass Slipper* (1924).

16. In 1924 Melchior Lengyel wrote *Antónia*, a comedy, for Sári Fedák, so that she could win a triumph over Lili Darvas. The incident is described in Chandler's book, p. 447.

17. *One, Two, Three* or *The President* (1929), *The Good Fairy* (1930), *Harmony* (1932), and *Arthur* (1932).

18. *Companion*, pp. 13, 67.

19. Ferenc Körmendy, "Egy Molnár történet," *Irodalmi Ujság*, 15 September 1961, p. 6.

20. The first TV production of Molnár's work was *Riviera* by Westinghouse in the "Studio One" series in 1950: publication of *Stories for Two*, collection of one-act plays (New York, 1950); and Molnár's *Romantic Comedies* (New York, 1952).

21. *New York Times*, 3 April 1952, p. 33.

22. Behrman, p. 253.

Chapter Three

1. Molnár, *All the Plays of Molnár* (New York, 1929), p. xv.

2. Molnár, "Decameron," *Ismerősök* (Budapest, 1917), pp. 207–209.

3. Contributor for *A Hét, Új Idők, Pesti Hirlap, Pesti Napló*, and *Fidibusz*, Budapest papers. He was also a reporter for the Hearst Papers and the *Berlin Tageblatt*.

4. Phillip Minoff, "Author in Exile," *Cue*, 28 January 1950, p. 16.

5. Sándor Bródy (1863–1924) was a popular novelist, essayist, and playwright; Molnár's mentor at first, later he became his ardent rival. Molnár dedicated *The Hungry City* to him and *Pipes of Pan* to his five sons.

6. Molnár, Foreword, *Ismerősök*, p. 137.

7. Bódog Halmi, *Molnár Ferenc az iró és az ember* (Budapest, 1929), p. 15.

8. Dezső Kosztolányi, "Molnár Ferenc," *Új Idők*, 9 December 1928, p. 70.

9. *Husbands and Lovers*, trans. Benjamin Glazer (New York, 1924); *Stories for Two*, no trans. *op. cit.*

10. The Hungarian title "Toll" means both pen and feather, as *Feder* in German.

11. Irén Vécsei, *Molnár Ferenc* (Budapest, 1966), p. 25.

12. Molnár, *A War Correspondent's Diary, 1914–15* (Budapest, 1916), p. 133.

13. Joseph Remenyi, "Ferenc Molnar, Hungarian Playwright," *Hungarian Writers and Literature* (New Brunswick, 1962), p. 354.

14. *The Captain of St. Margaret's,* see Chapter 7.

15. Remenyi, p. 355.

16. Miksa Fenyő, "*Muzsika.* Molnár Ferenc elbeszélései," *Nyugat* I (1908), 297.

17. Molnár, *Muzsika* (Budapest, 1908), p. 248.

18. *Ibid.,* p. 8.

19. *Ibid.,* p. 9.

20. George Halasz, *Molnár: The Man Behind the Monocle* (New York, 1929), p. 114.

Chapter Four

1. *Magdolna és egyéb elbeszélések,* Molnár's first book, was serialized by Gusztav Ranschburg and sold by subscription in 1898. The early short stories written abroad were collected under the title *A csókok éjszakája és egyéb elbeszélések* (Budapest, 1899).

2. Halmi, p. 28.

3. Aladár Schöpflin, *A magyar irodalom története a XX. században* (Budapest, 1937), p. 157.

4. *Az éhes város* (Budapest, 1901), p. 63.

5. Halasz, p. 63.

6. *Eva* and *The Derelict Boat,* trans. Emil Lengyel ((Indianapolis, 1926).

7. Hugó Csergő, "Hogyan lett Molnár Feriből Molnár Ferenc," biographical sketches serialized in *Magyar Hirlap* (1928).

8. *Eva* and *The Derelict Boat,* p. xiii.

9. *Fräulein Jourfix* (Leipzig, 1913).

10. *Prisoners,* trans. Joseph Szebenyei (Indianapolis, 1925); its movie version was released by Metro Pictures, 1929.

11. *The Paul Street Boys,* trans. Louis Rittenberg (New York, 1927); also appeared as *No Greater Glory* in the same year.

12. Dramatized in 1936 by Sándor Hevesi, in 1954 by Sándor Török; notable movie versions: *No Greater Glory,* 1934, directed by Frank Borzage; *The Paul Street Boys,* 1968, Hungarian-American co-production, directed by Zoltán Fábri.

13. *Tanulók Lapja,* ed. by Dr. Kornél Rupp, one of Molnár's high-school teachers.
14. *The Paul Street Boys,* p. 28.
15. *Ibid.,* p. 39.
16. *Ibid.,* p. 292.
17. Halmi, p. 49.
18. *Andor* (Budapest, 1918), p. 135.
19. Géza Hegedűs, Preface to Molnár's *Szinház* (Budapest, 1961), pp. 12–13.
20. Vécsei, p. 56.
21. György Lukács, *Magyar Irodalom-Magyar Kultura* (Budapest, 1970), p. 147.
22. *Angel making Music,* trans. Victor Katona and Peggy Barwell (New York, 1935), p. 279.
23. *Ibid.,* p. 12.
24. *Companion,* p. 222.
25. *Ibid.*
26. The book's translator, E. Lengyel, verifies that despite persistent promotion by Dr. Edmond Pauker, Molnár's New York agent, *Autumn Journey* was turned down by every publisher. (Personal interview with Professor Lengyel, 25 October 1977, in New York).

Chapter Five

1. Károly Kisfaludy (1788–1830), won critical acclaim by combining patriotic sentiment with effective dramaturgy in his widely popular, facile comedies.
2. Ede Szigligeti (1814–1878), writer of historical plays and comedies, was an able manager of the National Theater; Gergely Csíky (1842–1891), prolific playwright and dramaturge, influenced by the French *pièces à thèse,* became a favorite author of the emerging middle class.
3. Katona's *Bánk Bán* (1814), a profound historical tragedy, and Vörösmarty's symbolical, Romantic dramas were little known outside of Hungary; Madách's *Az ember tragédiája* (The Tragedy of Man) (1861), was a monumental philosophical work reminiscent of Goethe's *Faust.* It achieved some success abroad.
4. Chapter 3, Note 5.
5. *All the Plays of Molnár* (New York, 1929). Hereafter cited as *APM.* It contains twenty plays translated by various adapters.
6. Molnár refused to give the play to Beőthy's successor and instead of paying back the advance, he translated the play for the National Theater. For details, see Halasz, p. 77.

7. "A doktor úr," *Fővárosi Lapok*, November 29, 1902, p. 13.

8. *Molnár Ferenc Művei* (Budapest, 1928), Vol. 15, pp. 91–190.

9. Behrman, p. 218.

10. E. J. Gergely, *Hungarian Drama in New York* (Philadelphia, 1947), p. 13.

11. Gergely quoting Ryan Walker, *Arena*, December 1908, p. 536.

12. Gergely, p. 13, Note 8.

13. The play, translated by Philip Littel, produced by Harrison G. Fiske, received favorable critical notices but "the public didn't come; it was too subtle and too foreign to them." *Theatre Magazine*, 18 (October 1913), 115.

14. *Companion*, p. 118.

15. As quoted by Behrman, p. 223.

16. Ignotus, "A testőr," *Nyugat* II (1910), p. 1721.

17. Gergely, p. 31.

18. Zoltán Horváth, *Magyar századforduló* (Budapest, 1974), p. 417.

19. Most critics disparaged its "mundane theme," deeming the play "cynically divertive at a time of war." Halmi, p. 53.

20. The drama had eighty-six performances at the National Theater, and under a revised title, *Passions for Men*, it ran at the Belmont for two months. Gergely, p. 54.

21. "Molnár's Comedy of Sainthood," *New York Times*, 24 December 1922, Sec. 7, p. 1.

22. Gyula Krúdy, "Molnár és közönsége," *Magyarország*, No. 291, 1917, p. 27.

23. Edmund Wilson, "Budapest," *New Yorker*, 4 January 1966, p. 118.

24. Melville Baker's adaptation had 255 performances at the Court Theatre. Benjamin Glazer's translation, *The Swan*, was published by Boni & Liveright, 1923. The latter version was used in *APM*.

25. "Molnár's "The Swan," *New York Times*, 4 October 1923, p. 29.

26. *Theatre Magazine*, December 1923, p. 39.

27. Gergely, p. 45.

28. As part of a double bill with *One, Two, Three*, it opened at the Henry Miller Theatre and closed after forty performances. The *New York Times* dismissed it as "a cheap, third-rate piece," 30 September 1930, p. 24.

29. "Tales of Manhattan" with other authors in 1932; "Magnificent Lie" in 1931; its TV version featured Lee Tracy in 1951; "If You Can

Act—Act" in 1960. It was published in a later collection as "Actor from Vienna" in *Romantic Comedies.*

30. Chapter 4, Part III.

31. The Hungarian critics called it "a pathetic, improbable love story," as quoted by Sándor Hunyady, *Álmatlan éjjel* (Budapest, 1970), p. 194. In New York it closed after thirteen performances—a humiliating box-office failure for Molnár. The *New York Times* called it "a cynical, sacrilegious, phoney spectacle of a neurasthenic lunatic," 11 October 1923, p. 16.

32. *Theatre Magazine*, December 1923, p. 16.

33. Aurél Kárpáti's Preface to the Hungarian translation of *Companion in Exile* (*Utitárs a száműzetésben*) (Budapest, 1958), p. 15.

34. Louis Rittenberg quoting Molnár in the Preface of *APM*, p. xxi.

35. Chandler, p. 448.

36. Chapter 2, Note 18.

37. Critics called Philip Moeller's adaption "a drab nauseating tale, a trifling comedy, offensive everywhere," Gergely, p. 41.

38. Halmi, p. 71.

39. Lili Darvas recalls how she was preparing for her first role in German; she was to play Louise in the Vienna performance of *Riviera*, directed by Max Reinhardt. She was practicing her German pronunciation with a voice teacher when the famous misunderstanding occurred that inspired *The Play's the Thing*. "Erőss András meséli," *Menora*, 8 June 1977, p. 11.

40. Péter Nagy, "Molnár Ferenc szinpada," *Irodalomtörténet*, 1978, I, p. 74.

41. Dezső Kosztolányi, "Riviera," *Pesti Hírlap*, 13 January 1926, p. 15.

42. Rittenberg, Introduction to *APM*, p. xxi.

43. Gergely, p. 55. After 326 performances on Broadway, the play toured the country.

44. On Easter Sunday 1928, the play ran in fifty theaters in Germany alone. George Middleton, *These Things Are Mine* (New York, 1947), p. 366. The London production also opened in 1928.

45. Aladár Schöpflin, *Válogatott irodalmi tanulmányok* (Budapest, 1967), p. 564.

46. "Molnár's Necromancy," *New York Times*, 14 November 1926, Sec. 8, p. 1.

47. Statistics provided by Magyar Szinháztörténeti Intézet, Budapest.

48. *His Glorious Night* in 1929, *A Breath of Scandal* in 1960;

MGM also produced the first version in German, French, and Spanish in 1930.

49. Aladár Schöpflin, "Olympia," *Nyugat* I (1928), p. 468.

50. *New York Times*, 17 October 1928, p. 26.

51. Behrman, p. 231.

52. Péter Nagy, "Szinházi levél," *Élet és Irodalom*, 8 May 1965, p. 5.

53. Vera Létay, "Olympia," *Népszabadság*, 3 May 1965.

54. *Romantic Comedies* (New York, 1952); henceforth page numbers refer to this volume. It contains six new plays and the revised version of *Marshal* and *Anniversary Dinner*, a one-acter originally written in 1917. Hereafter cited as *RC*.

55. The *RC* version changed the characters' names and the heroine's nationality into Swedish; otherwise the text is identical with Sydney Howard's able translation used at the Henry Miller Theatre.

56. *New York Times*, 30 September 1930, p. 24.

57. Vécsei, p. 101.

58. Jane Hinton's adaptation opened on November 24, 1931 at the Henry Miller Theatre and ran 151 times; on November 17, 1932, it reopened and had sixty-eight shows. *New York Times*, 25 November 1931, p. 17, "Molnar seems to be bored lately and boggles his job as an artist." *Theatre Arts Monthly*, Feb. 1932, p. 98, referred to it as "a perilously weak script with a mere feeling of a play . . . an accomplishment to meet a half play half way and succeeding."

59. Universal Pictures produced *The Good Fairy* in 1935, and *I'll Be Yours* in 1947; both based on the play's script.

60. Counterpoint Theatre Company, directed by Howard Green.

61. *Companion*, p. 137.

62. My own translation. *Harmónia* (Budapest, 1932), pp. 127–28.

63. The typescript, translated by Emil Lengyel and George Nathan, is available in the New York Public Library.

64. *Csoda a hegyek közt* (Budapest, 1933), p. 142.

65. Béla Osváth, "A Molnár legenda," *Kritika*, September 1963, I, p. 45.

66. Mihály Babits, *Könyvről könyvre* (Budapest, 1973), p. 179.

67. Kárpáti, Preface, p. 34.

68. *New York Theatre Critics*, 26 April 1947, p. 387.

69. *Companion*, p. 125.

70. Completely revised, it was made into a movie, *The Bride Wore Red*, by MGM in 1937. The script is in the Pauker Collection at Yale.

71. A short scene portraying the behind-the-scenes bargaining of

two fathers-in-law about the dowry. It was not produced in America; the English translation by Barrows Mussey is in the Pauker Collection.
72. *Delicate Story,* trans. Gilbert Miller (New York, 1941), p. 122.
73. *New York Post,* 5 December 1940, p. 37.
74. *Delicate Story,* pp. 49–50.
75. *Ibid.,* p. 56.
76. *Double Wedding,* screenplay by Swerling and Walso Salt (Culver City, Calif., 1937). Rough translation of the original script is in the Pauker Collection.
77. *Blond Fever,* produced by MGM in 1944.

Chapter Six

1. Chapter 3, Part IV.
2. As an example, Behrman recalls (p. 214) that in Germany, in the early 1920s, *Liliom* was being played in 200 theaters the same week.
3. The adapter made only a few changes: he added a prologue to show the Budapest environment and the amusement park; he also made Mrs. Hollunder Julie's aunt (she had been Liliom's relative in the original), to emphasize the growing pressure on the hero.
4. The *National Union Catalogue* lists twenty-four different editions of *Liliom* in various languages. The text used here is the Glazer adaptation published in *APM.*
5. Molnár's Preface to the *Playbill* for the 1909 production.
6. Halasz, p. 97.
7. Gregory Stragnell, M.D., "A Psychopathological Study of Franz Molnár's Liliom," *Psychoanalytical Review,* 9 (January 1922), pp. 40–49.
8. *Ibid.,* p. 49.
9. Kárpáti, Preface, p. 12.
10. *History of Hungarian Literature* (Budapest, 1964), p. 221.
11. Halasz, p. 98.
12. Nagy, *Irodalomtörténet,* 1978, I p. 51.
13. Benjamin Glazer's Preface to *Liliom* (New York, 1921).
14. Alfred Kerr, "Liliom," *Berliner Tageblatt,* November 17, 1922.
15. Miksa Fenyő, "Liliom," *Nyugat,* II (1909), p. 674.
16. Nagy, *op. cit.,* pp. 52–53.
17. Endre Illés, *Krétarajzok* (Budapest, 1957), pp. 446–47.
18. Gassner, p. 480.
19. Chandler, p. 441.
20. Remenyi, p. 359.

21. Brooks Atkinson, "A Revival of Ferenc Molnar's *Liliom*," *New York Times*, 26 March 1940.

Chapter Seven

1. Behrman, p. 251.
2. Miklós Lázár, "Molnár Ferenc new yorki élete és halála," *Manuscript* (New York, 1962), p. 18.
3. *The Blue-Eyed Lady* (New York, 1942). In Hungarian, *A kékszemű* (Budapest, 1957).
4. *Farewell My Heart* (New York, 1945); *Isten veled szivem* (Budapest, 1947).
5. *Companion*, p. 264.
6. Lukács, p. 434.
7. *Farewell My Heart*, p. 85.
8. *Ibid.*, p. 159.
9. *The Captain of St. Margaret's*, trans. Barrows Mussey (New York, 1945). The British edition appeared as *Captain Magnificent* (London, 1946).
10. Ostensibly submitted as "Notes for an Autobiography."
11. Mrs. Bartha's list of Molnár's meetings with famous people; his friendship with Puccini, Bergson, Jacobi, Bruno Walter, Gershwin, Chagall, Billy Rose, Gilbert Miller, David Belasco, Morris Gest, Moss Hart, Edna Ferber, and scores of other now legendary theatrical personalities, may provide valuable material for biographers. *Companion*, pp. 244–47.
12. *Companion*, p. 264.
13. *Ibid.*, p. 363.
14. *Ibid.*, p. 362.
15. *King's Maid's* first performance took place on August 25, 1941, at Bass Rocks Theater, Gloucester, Mass., produced by Oscar Serling; on November 24, 1941, it opened at the Maryland Theater, Baltimore, Md. The play, unknown in Hungary, was never published; typescripts are at the New York Public Library, Lincoln Center Annex.
16. *Companion*, p. 37.
17. Included in the Pauker Collection deposited at Yale, copyright 1942.
18. *Merciless Mrs. Roy* has the same plot but names and ranks of characters are different; to *Waxwork* Molnár also added the Prologue.
19. Molnár's stage direction to *Waxwork*; *RC*, p. 83.
20. The play only exists in MS form in the New York Public

Library, Lincoln Center Annex. The Hungarian typescript, "A császár," belongs to the Petőfi Museum.

21. *The Emperor*, playscript, Act. 2, page 8.

22. Vécsei quoting Áron Tamási's review in *Szinház*, 26 April 1946, p. 132.

23. Never published or adapted; the English MS, prepared by Molnár himself, is in the Pauker Collection.

24. Included in *RC*, pp. 283–331. The other versions are in the Pauker collection. In 1952, it was staged in Kiel, Germany, but failed after ten performances; the 1971 opening in Vienna fared no better. In Hungary it exists only in typescript, "Szivdobogás," stored in Irodalomtörténeti Intézet.

25. The two English manuscripts in longhand contain the same type of corrections by the same colored ink as in *Noah's Ark*. All copies are in the New York Public Library, Lincoln Center Annex.

26. It opened on February 15, 1961, at Theater Marquee in John Bettenbender's adaptation.

27. Every version is in the Pauker Collection.

28. *Girl of My Dreams* was televised in the Westinghouse series "Studio One." All the translations are in the Pauker Collection.

29. *Companion*, pp. 343–44.

Chapter Eight

1. David Belasco, "An Appreciation," Introduction to Molnár's *AMP*, p. IX.

2. Personal interview with Robert Brustein, 27 January 1978.

3. Molnár, *The Swan*, APM, p. 410.

Selected Bibliography

(Place of publication is Budapest unless otherwise noted.)

PRIMARY SOURCES

1. Collected Editions

Molnár Ferenc művei, 20 vols. Franklin-Társulat, 1928.
Szinház: Szinművek, introd. Géza Hegedüs. Szépirodalmi Könyvkiadó, 1961.
Szülőfalum, Pest, ed. Irén Vécsei. Szépirodalmi Könyvkiadó, 1962.

2. Individual Editions

(Includes the most important works that appeared in Molnár's lifetime. Dates refer to first editions in book form.)

a. Novels

Az éhes város. Révai és Salamon, 1901.
Egy gazdátlan csónak története. Magyar Hírlap, 1901.
Éva. Magyar Hírlap, 1903.
Egy pesti lány története. Magyar Kereskedelmi Közlöny, 1905.
A Pál-utcai fiúk. Franklin-Társulat, 1907.
Rabok. Franklin-Társulat, 1908.
Andor. Athenaeum, 1918.
A zenélő angyal. Athenaeum, 1933.
A zöld huszár. Athenaeum, 1937.
Őszi utazás. Athenaeum, 1939.
Isten veled szivem. Káldor György, 1947.

b. Stories, Essays, Sketches, and Editorials

Magdolna és egyéb elbeszélések. Ranschburg, 1898.
A csókok éjszakája és egyéb elbeszélések. V. Kunosy, 1899.
Gyerekek. R. Lampel, 1905.
Muzsika. Franklin-Társulat, 1908.
Ketten beszélnek. Franklin-Társulat, 1909.
Pesti erkölcsök. R. Lampel, 1909.

Hétágú síp. Franklin-Társulat, 1911.
Ma, tegnap, tegnapelőtt. R. Lampel, 1912.
Báró Márczius és egyéb elbeszélések. R. Lampel, 1913.
Kis hármaskönyv. Franklin-Társulat, 1914.
Az aruvimi erdő titka és egyéb szatirák. Légrády Testvérek, 1916.
Egy haditudósitó emlékei. Franklin-Társulat, 1916.
Ismerősök. Franklin-Társulat, 1917.
Széntolvajok. Népszava, 1918.
Gőzoszlop. Franklin-Társulat, 1924.

c. Plays

A doktor úr. R. Lampel, 1902.
Józsi. R. Lampel, 1904.
Az ördög. Franklin-Társulat, 1907.
Liliom. Franklin-Társulat, 1910.
A testőr. Franklin-Társulat, 1910.
A farkas. Franklin-Társulat, 1912.
Farsang. Franklin-Társulat, 1917.
Úri divat. Franklin-Társulat, 1917.
A hattyú. Franklin-Társulat, 1921.
Szinház: Előjáték Lear királyhoz, Marsall, Az ibolya. Franklin-Társulat, 1921.
Égi és földi szerelem. Pantheon, 1922.
A vörös malom. Franklin-Társulat, 1923.
Az üvegcipő. Franklin-Társulat, 1924.
Játék a kastélyban. Franklin-Társulat, 1926.
Riviera. Franklin-Társulat, 1926.
Olympia. Franklin-Társulat, 1928.
Egy-kettő-három. Franklin-Társulat, 1929.
A jó tündér. Athenaeum, 1930.
Harmónia. Athenaeum, 1932.
Valaki. Franklin-Társulat, 1932.
Csoda a hegyek közt. Athenaeum, 1933.
Az ismeretlen lány. Athenaeum, 1934.
Nagy szerelem. Athenaeum, 1935.
Delila. Athenaeum, 1937.

3. English Translations—Collected Editions

All the Plays of Molnár, introd. David Belasco, ed. Louis Rittenberg. New York: The Vanguard Press, 1929; rpt. New York: Garden City, 1937.

Romantic Comedies: Eight Plays by Ferenc Molnár. New York: Crown, 1952.

MOLNÁR, FERENC. *Husbands and Lovers,* trans. Benjamin Glazer. New York: Boni & Liveright, 1924.

MOLNÁR, FERENC. *Stories for Two.* New York: Horizon, 1950.

The Captain of St. Margaret's: Twenty-five Chapters of Memoires, trans. Barrows Mussey. New York: Duell, Sloan & Pearce, 1945.

4. English Translations—Individual Editions

(There were numerous English translations of both Molnár's novels and plays. This section includes only the most important ones.)

a. Novels

Eva and *The Derelict Boat,* trans. Emil Lengyel. Indianapolis: Bobbs-Merrill, 1924.

Prisoners, trans. Joseph Szebenyei. Indianapolis: Bobbs-Merrill, 1924.

The Paul Street Boys, trans. Louis Rittenberg. New York: Masi-Masius, 1927.

Angel making Music, trans. Victor Katona and Peggy Barwell. New York: H. Smith & R. Haas, 1935.

Farewell My Heart, trans. Elinor Rice. New York: Simon and Schuster, 1945.

Companion in Exile: Notes for an Autobiography, trans. Barrows Mussey. New York: Gaer Associates, 1950.

b. Plays

The Devil, trans. Oliver Herford. New York: K. Kennerley, 1908.

Liliom, trans. Benjamin Glazer. New York: Boni and Liveright, 1921.

The Guardsman, trans. Grace I. Cobron and Hans Bartsch. New York: Boni and Liveright, 1924.

The Swan, trans. Melville Baker. New York: Longmans, Green & Co., 1929.

The Play's the Thing, trans. P. G. Wodehouse. New York: Brentano's, 1927.

Olympia, trans. Sydney Howard. New York:: Brentano's, 1928.

The Good Fairy, trans. Jane Hinton. New York: Long and Smith, Inc., 1932.

Delicate Story, trans. Gilbert Miller. New York: Samuel French, 1941.

SECONDARY SOURCES

1. Books

GERGELY, EMRO J. *Hungarian Drama in New York: American Adaptations 1908–1940.* Philadelphia: Univ. of Pennsylvania Press, 1947. Excellent critical analysis of sixteen Molnár plays produced on Broadway.

HALASZ, GEORGE. *Ferenc Molnár: The Man Behind the Monocle.* New York: n.p., 1929. Fair early account of Molnár's development as an artist, with special emphasis on his colorful life.

HALMI, BÓDOG. *Molnár Ferenc az iró és az ember.* Budapest: by the author, 1929. Unfavorably biased study of Molnár's place in Hungarian literature, with brief criticism of his major works between 1900–1927.

MOLNÁR, ERZSÉBET. *Testvérek voltunk.* Budapest: Magvető, 1958. Personal memoirs of his sister about their relationship. It describes their childhood but provides no particular insights.

VÉCSEI, IRÉN. *Molnár Ferenc.* Budapest: Gondolat, 1966. An unevenly written monograph, the first Marxist analysis of Molnár's art, highly critical of its apolitical nature.

2. Articles

BEHRMAN, S. N. "Playwright: Ferenc Molnár," *The Suspended Drawing Room.* New York: Stein & Day Publishers, 1965, pp. 191–253. Amusing biographical sketch filled with Molnár anecdotes and some play analyses.

CHANDLER, FRANK W. "Hungarian and Czech Innovators: Molnár and the Capeks," *Modern Continental Playwrights.* New York: Harper & Brothers, 1931, pp. 438–53. Good general summary of ten early plays of Molnár.

FENYŐ, MIKSA. "*Muzsika.* Molnár Ferenc elbeszélései." *Nyugat,* I (1908), 279–92. Excellent general introduction with sensitive interpretation of Molnár's first short-story collection.

GASSNER, JOHN. "Molnar and the Hungarians," *Masters of the Drama.* New York: Dover Publications, 1945, pp. 478–81. Succinct account of Molnár's contribution to drama, with special emphasis on *Liliom.*

GYÁRFÁS, MIKLÓS. "Vita a Molnár-legendával," *Új Irás,* III (1963), 1384–87. A special rebuttal to Osváth's article (below), proving that Molnár belongs to the great masters of Hungarian drama.

HAJDU, GYŐZŐ. "Elhervadt-e a *Liliom?*" *Műhely.* Bucharest: Irodalmi

Könyvkiadó, 1967, pp. 359–72. Somewhat biased, Marxist analysis of *Liliom.*

HEGEDŰS, GÉZA, and KÓNYA, JUDITH. *A magyar dráma útja.* Budapest: Gondolat Kiadó, 1964, pp. 153–58. Highly readable but questionable discussion of the various stages of Molnár's development.

HORVÁTH, ZOLTÁN. *Magyar századforduló.* 2nd ed. Budapest: Gondolat Kiadó, 1974. Highly critical account of Molnár's work and its impact on Hungarian literature.

ILLÉS, ENDRE. "A fiatal Molnár Ferenc," *Krétarajzok.* Budapest: Magvető, 1957, pp. 316–19. Brief but useful observations about Molnár's early prose pieces with special emphasis on *The Paul Street Boys.*

KÁRPÁTI, AURÉL. "Molnár Ferenc. Mozaik," *Tegnaptól Máig.* Budapest: Szépirodalmi Könyvkiadó, 1961, pp. 183–220. Different studies dealing with Molnár's development as a dramatist providing excellent insights to his controversial personality and some of his works.

KLANICZAY, TIBOR; SZABOLCSI, MIKLÓS; and SZANDER, JÓZSEF. *History of Hungarian Literature.* Budapest: Corvina Press, 1964. Good background material, summary of Hungary's literary climate during Molnár's career.

LUKÁCS GYÖRGY. *Magyar Irodalom–Magyar Kultura.* Budapest: Gondolat Kiadó, 1970, pp. 143–48, 433–38. Interesting but highly critical accounts of *Andor* and *Farewell My Heart.*

MIDDLETON, GEORGE. *These Things Are Mine.* New York: The Macmillan Co., 1947, pp. 363–69. Intimate portrait of Molnár in the 1920s, with emphasis on his appeal as a dramatist in Europe.

NAGY, GEORGE L. "Ferenc Molnárs Stücke auf der Deutschsprachigen Bühne." Diss., State University of N.Y. at Albany, 1978. Fine biographical and critical account of the entire Molnár *oeuvre* with special emphasis on the reception of his plays in Germany and Austria.

NAGY, PÉTER. "Molnár Ferencről," *Irodalomtörténet,* 48 (1960), 377–82. Intelligent, sober, critical interpretation of some of Molnár's major short stories and *Companion in Exile.*

———. "Molnár Ferenc szinpada," *Irodalomtörténet,* I (1978), 32–84. Well-researched, detailed analysis of Molnár's plays and their critical reception in Hungary.

OSVÁTH, BÉLA. "A Molnár-legenda," *Kritika,* I (1963), 40–46. Extremely biased, Marxist criticism of Molnár's plays. It refutes the Molnár legend by stating that his inferior plays made the audience insensitive to truly modern theater.

REMENYI, JÓZSEF. "Ferenc Molnar, Hungarian Playwright," *Hungarian Writers and Literature*. New Brunswick, N.J.: Rutgers University Press, 1964, pp. 348–62. Thorough general introduction with highly critical account of Molnár's major works.

SCHÖPFLIN, ALADÁR. "Molnár Ferenc," *Válogatott tanulmányok*. Budapest: Szépirodalmi Könyvkiadó, 1967, pp. 562–65, 572–77. Complimentary evaluation of Molnár as the only Hungarian writer of international reputation.

SZÁSZ, KÁROLY. "Molnár Ferenc mint drámairó," *Iradalomtörténet*, 18 (1929), 151–60. Unfairly critical evaluation of sixteen Molnár plays up to 1929.

WILSON, EDMUND. "Hungary," *New Yorker*, 4 June 1966, pp. 110–39. Useful survey of Molnár's appeal, with detailed analyses of *The Devil* and *Fashions for Man*.

Index

DATE DUE

DEMCO 38-297